villa
cookbook
d'este

vild

cookbook

jean govoni salvadore

RECIPES BY LUCIANO PAROLARI · PHOTOGRAPHS BY GIORGIO PIZZI

S EDITIONS

This edition published in 2004 by Villa d'Este

Distributed by Villa d'Este
22012 Cernobbio - Lago di Como - Italy
Tel. +39 031.3481 - Fax +39 031.348844
www.villadeste.it - e-mail:info@villadeste.it

Printed in Italy by Brunati Arti Grafiche
22020 S. Fermo - Como - Italy
Tel. +39 031.210554 - Fax +39 031.212058
e-mail:info@brunatiartigrafiche.com - www.brunatiartigrafiche.com

ISBN: 1-55670-B81-5

Design: Jennie Chang for Divine Design Studio. Inc.

acknowledgments

When I was very young, I would look forward to visiting my grandparents in their country home in Campogalliano, outside of Modena. It was a big treat to spend time in the kitchen and watch the cooks assemble the tortellini. I was fascinated to see how they were prepared: the dough was made by hand and then rolled out, cut up, and stuffed with a filling of meat, prosciutto, mortadella, parmesan cheese, and egg. In no time, tortellini, tortelloni, and ravioli were turned out by the hundreds.

Both of my parents' families came from the region of Emilia. The natives of this region are strong, hardworking, warmblooded, hearty eaters and, above all, have a zest for life and a love for food which I am sure I have inherited. Wherever my family took up residence—in London, Paris, or Rome—I developed a genuine interest in the cuisine of the country in which we lived.

Thirty years ago, I moved to Villa d'Este. Shortly thereafter, we began teaching cooking classes here. In 1990, we decided to put together a cookbook with Luciano Parolari's recipes and Giorgio Pizzi's photographs. Printed by our local printer Carlo Brunati, it was available only at Villa d'Este. I am indebted to Jean-Marc Droulers, Mario Arrigo, and Claudio Ceccherelli for their caring guidance. For deciding to make the book available to a larger audience, I am grateful to Marta Hallett at S Editions. Gabrielle Pecarsky edited the book and oversaw its new, spectacular design.

It is impossible to list all the friends who encouraged and supported me, as I have to go back several decades, beginning with Helen McCully, James Beard, the Kriendlers of the '21' Club, Jane Montant, Camille Glenn, Julie Dannenbaum, Chuck Williams, Natale Rusconi, Steven Kaufmann, Larry Ashmead, Fred Laubi, Pamela Fiori, Giulano Bugialli, Sissie Morris, and Marty Schott.

I must not forget my Australian friends: Mary Rossi, Leo Schofield, Jerry Henderson, and Beverley Sutherland-Smith, just to mention a few names. Their contributions have been invaluable. Last but not least, my silent partner Annamaria Duvia, who has deciphered all of my scribbles and scrawls. Without her, this book never would have seen the light.

And in loving memory to Luca Salvadore, my husband of forty years, who lived to eat.

contents

The world-famous sixteenth century Villa d'Este mosaic provides a perfect setting for the array of fresh vegetables that garnish most of the Villa d'Este dishes.

An unusual view of the Villa d'Este seen from the water. Overlooking the lakefront with the luxuriant gardens in the background and the hills of the village of Cernobbio rising above, the two hotel properties suddenly appear as if by magic. On the left, the Cardinal's Building, and on the right, the Queen's Pavilion.

A SPECTACULAR GARDEN VIEW FROM THE VERANDAH
RESTAURANT, THE FORMAL DINING ROOM OF VILLA D'ESTE.

introduction

The idea of starting a cooking school on the shores of Lake Como goes back nearly thirty years. By 1973, when Villa d'Este celebrated its 100th anniversary as a hotel, cooking classes were in full swing. Word circulated and groups from the United States and Australia crowded the kitchens of Villa d'Este. In 1976, Julie Dannenbaum invited Luciano Parolari, our executive chef, and Jean Salvadore, our public relations manager, to be guests at her cooking school in Philadelphia. Thanks to Julie, who initiated that first visit, Luciano and Jean traveled repeatedly to the United States during the winter months, when the hotel was closed, giving demonstrations for various benefit events. As expected, the Villa d'Este recipes were in great demand by both new initiates and former visitors alike.

Our first publishing venture was a Christmas card containing a full menu, followed, in 1981, by the book *Cooking Ideas from the Villa d'Este*, available only at the hotel. Jean Salvadore compiled the book by adapting the chef's recipes and adding some of her own—all very simple recipes to prepare.

We continued to mail our Christmas menus, and because we received so many favorable comments, we decided to offer this new cookbook with beautiful color photographs accompanying each recipe. We have also included photographs of the Villa d'Este restaurants and other eating sites about the hotel and its surroundings, hoping that our guests will take home a souvenir of their stay on Lake Como and that those who visit the hotel through the book will soon visit in person.

In the last ten years, there have been many changes in the way people eat. Everyone is concerned about putting on weight, reducing the intake of calories and cholesterol levels. With this in mind, our Villa d'Este chefs substitute oil for butter when possible, and they cook with wine and herbs to enhance the flavors. As a result, the food is lighter and healthier.

Italian food has become trendy, and the numerous Italian restaurants that are popping up all over the world, especially in the United States, are considered very "in." Twenty or thirty years ago, Italian cuisine was known abroad only for spaghetti and meatballs. Only when tourists started flocking to Italy did they discover that Italians "at home" ate quite differently from what was considered Italian food in their countries. Extra-virgin olive oil, Parmesan cheese (Parmigiano Reggiano), white truffles (only available in Alba, Piedmont), saffron risottos, porcini mushrooms, Florentine T-bone steak, the most tender veal, prosciutto crudo, baby lambs that have not yet tasted a blade of grass, red radicchio salad from Treviso, asparagus, and artichokes are only a few of the items that are considered basic ingredients for the refined palate in Northern Italy. The truth is that we Italians enjoy our food so much that we can be quite extravagant in preparing our meals. Italian cooking is based on quality ingredients, which is why it is considered one of the most expensive in the gastronomic world.

The recipes in our revised cookbook are still the traditional ones, and great care has been taken in the presentation of the dishes. The wonderful photographs by Giorgio Pizzi will inspire every chef to try these dishes at home. Luciano Parolari, our executive chef, and his assistants, Cesare Chessorti, the chef of our Grill restaurant, and Natalino Michielli, the pastry chef, beautifully styled and cooked the enticing array of foods here. And Jean Salvadore edited and compiled the distinctive recipes. We hope that our friends will enjoy reading and cooking from the book as much as we at Villa d'Este enjoyed putting it together.

JEAN-MARC DROULERS
Chief Executive Officer, Villa d'Este

Past the fabulous

lobby—with its sparkling crystal chan-
deliers, white marble columns, vaulted
hallways, and double staircases—is the
statue *Venus Crowned by Eros*, attrib-
uted to the sculptor Antonio Canova.

A PAINTING OF VILLA D'ESTE AS SEEN IN 1815, WHEN
THE QUEEN OF ENGLAND PURCHASED THE PROPERTY.

historical notes

The history of Villa d'Este dates back more than 500 years, when Cernobbio, a small village, was populated by fishermen and woodcutters. Nuns taking refuge from the civil war in a church, where today you find the park of Villa d'Este, were the first to arrive on the site where the hotel compound now stands.

Nearby Como, already a thriving city, famous in the sixteenth century for its silk manufacturing, is still the major industry of the area. One of its leading families of that period were the Ottavio Gallios, whose youngest son, Tolomeo, studied in Rome and, at age 38, returned to Como as cardinal of the city, under the papacy of Pius IV. It was at this point that the Gallios, having acquired the old cloister of Sant' Andrea and an extension of the surrounding land, decided to build a villa on the lakeshore, at the time considered extremely fashionable. One of the most accomplished architects of the time was Pellegrino Pellegrini of Valsolda, to whom Cardinal Tolomeo Gallio commissioned the planning. The villa, named "Garrovo," after the mountain stream that flows into the lake, was built in 1568 and was considered one of the finest examples of architecture and landscaping.

After the cardinal's death, Villa Garrovo was inherited by a nephew, Tolomeo, duke of Alvito, who continued to embellish the house and the gardens in Renaissance style. Its fame reached far and wide. In 1614, the sultan of Morocco, accompanied by his retinue, arrived in Cernobbio with the sole purpose of visiting the villa and seeing for himself its reported splendors.

For more than two centuries, the House of Gallio reigned uncontested on the shores of Cernobbio, until the latter part of the eighteenth century, when one of the descendants of Tolomeo Gallio moved to Naples, and the family began to lose interest in the property.

In 1782, Carlo Tolomeo Gallio Trivulzio, duke of Alvito, sold the estate to Count Ruggero Marliani, a colonel of the Austrian army and delegate to the government of Lombardy; but only two years later, the villa had a new proprietor, Marquis Bartolomeo Calderara, a dissolute and affluent aristocrat who squandered a fortune in wine, women, and song and allowed the Villa to fall into a state of disrepair.

The ensuing renovation of Villa Garrovo was initiated by the aged Milanese playboy Marquis Calderara, who had married Vittoria Peluso, a famous ballerina of the time, nicknamed "Pelusina." It was said that the marchioness was not accepted by the aristocracy of Milan because she was considered to be a "social climber" even though "Pelusina" pirouetted on the La Scala stage. La Pelusina decided to ignore these slights and undertook to build up her image to compete with the noble families of Lombardy.

After the marquis died, Donna Vittoria, still young and attractive, wasted no time in remarrying. Her choice was a handsome young Napoleonic general, Count Domenico Pino. Thinking that he might suffer from war nostalgia, she had a series of simulated fortresses and towers built on the slopes overlooking the gardens. The general was so delighted with these structures that he recruited a group of military cadets to play mock battles, after which lucullian meals were served, champagne flowed abundantly, and fireworks went off. The fortress walls are still standing in the gardens of Villa d'Este today.

A turning point in Villa d'Este's history occurred in 1815, when Caroline of Brunswick-Wolfenbüttel, Princess of Wales and future queen of England, acquired Villa d'Este. This was, without a doubt, one of the most interesting chapters in the history of the villa, which she renamed the "New Villa d'Este."

It was known that the Princess of Wales lived almost in exile because she was incompatible with her husband, George IV, who was also her first cousin. He repudiated her shortly after their wedding, which had been arranged solely to pay off his debts, replenish his finances, and obtain a legitimate heir. Caroline left the conjugal roof and traveled throughout Europe without a fixed residence. When she discovered Lake Como in 1814, it was love at first sight. Many books, full of slanderous things, have been written about the tragic figure of Caroline, so it pleases us today to learn that she spent the happiest time of her troubled life on Lake Como.

In 1815, Caroline, determined to purchase the estate of Garrovo, rented a villa—soon to be Villa d'Este—in Como. The following year, Countess Pino condescended to a sale only because it was a royal wish. She insisted that this wish should be expressed in the deed of sale. The Pinos then took up residence at Villa Cima, which is the first building one passes on the right after entering the gates of Villa d'Este.

Once in ownership of the villa, Princess Caroline changed the name to "New Villa d'Este." The connection with the Este family was very remote, but research reveals that the House of Brunswick, to which Caroline belonged, and the House of Hanover, from which her estranged husband descended, both originated from a certain Guelfo d'Este, who left Germany for Italy in 1504. For five years, Caroline d'Este dedicated herself to decorating her beloved residence.

The gossip columns of the times reported that she led a dissolute life and that her parties were veritable orgies, but the columns were certainly exaggerated to discredit her in the eyes of her future subjects, who nevertheless continued to adore her. The calumny was mostly due to the continued presence of her chamberlain, Bartolomeo Pergami, baron of Franchina, a good-looking young man who was introduced to her by Count Pino. She was also popular among the people of Cernobbio, to whom she was extremely generous; in particular, we should be grateful to her because, among her many innovations is the road constructed between Como and Cernobbio.

However, this lavish and extravagant tenure of life indebted the princess to her banker, Prince Torlonia of Rome, so when in 1820 she returned to London in an abortive attempt to take her place on the throne, she left the Villa d'Este deed of sale in the hands of her banker with the understanding that she would get it back by paying her debts. But Caroline was never to return. She died heartbroken in 1821, after the scandalous divorce action filed against her by the king. A long period of inactivity at the villa followed.

In 1825, Louis Viganò published a guidebook to Villa d'Este, attracting hordes of tourists and souvenir hunters to Lake Como to see the famous villa and its gardens. Unfortunately, this did not contribute to its preservation. In 1829, the heirs of the banker Prince Torlonia sold the property to Prince Domenico Orsini, who resold it to Baron Ippolito Ciani in 1834.

Ciani, who had served as aide-de-camp to Napoleon and had been given the title of baron by the emperor, was responsible for restoring the estate with loving care. In 1856, he built a new villa on the premises and named it in honor of Caroline of Brunswick: "Hotel de la Reine d'Angleterre." The plan was to launch it as a spa. Overlooking the lake and located beyond the 500-year-old plane tree, it is now known as the Queen's Building.

The most glorious page in the history of Villa d'Este was written during Ciani's permanence on the shores of Lake Como, when Milan and all of Lombardy were still under Austrian domination, although the insurrection was already under way. This is when Villa d'Este underwent another transformation: The return of frivolous parties and banquets, used as a cover-up for the patriotic activities of those involved in the preparation of the "Five days of Milan" (March 18-22, 1848), during the period of the Italian Risorgimento, which culminated in 1870, when Italy was finally united as one country.

Another glamorous page was added in 1868, when Empress Maria Fedorowna of the Russian czar rented the villa for a two-month period and stayed on for two years. The mild, pleasant climate and the peaceful, relaxing atmosphere of the lake so became the czarina that she settled down very happily to a new way of life. Beloved because of her kindness and dedication to charitable works, her sudden return to Russia in 1873 was a cause of great sadness to the inhabitants of the village. At this time, a group of ingenious businessmen formed a limited company known as Villa d'Este, and they combined the two villas into one property: the Cardinal's and the Queen's. Villa d'Este was to become famous as a luxury hotel all over the world.

The first major improvement organized by the new owners was to build a terrace overlooking the lake; originally, the facade of the villa rose directly out of the water. After that came a succession of carefully planned additions. In 1926, the famous Villa d'Este eighteen-hole golf course and clubhouse were inaugurated at Montorfano. Only seven miles from the hotel, they are considered one of the finest and most challenging ever designed.

During the last thirty-five years, Villa d'Este has undergone a complete streamlining to provide up-to-date service. The cuisine has been prepared for a diversity of tastes.

There are three restaurants on the hotel's grounds. There is a formal dining room and covered Verandah with electronically controlled glass screens; the Grill, with its informal milieu, and in the summer, outdoor lunches around the pool and dinners in the gardens; and Kisho, an haute-cuisine Japanese restaurant. Pleasant entertainment is provided in a nightclub featuring a band with a singer; a discotheque; and the Canova Room, with a pianist. Gorgeous photographs of these locales are sprinkled throughout the cookbook, showing the environments in which Villa d'Este's world-class cuisine is offered.

Open from March until November, Villa d'Este can be reached by car or train in less than forty-five minutes from Milan; its fabulous cuisine offers refreshment for local inhabitants and tourists alike. Less than three hours from the ski resort of Saint Moritz, and only a few minutes from the Swiss border, it is considered the "in" place for guests of all ages and tastes.

THE CANOVA BAR, WITH MARBLE STATUES OF ADAM AND EVE COMMIS-
SIONED IN THE SIXTEENTH CENTURY BY CARDINAL TOLOMEO GALLIO.

Antipasto (hors d'oeuvres) means "before the meal," and in Italy it is served at the table only on special occasions. Traditionally, it consists of various types of salami, prosciutto crudo, and sometimes bresaola. In the photo, a corner view of the vaulted cellars where the salamis, mortadellas, sausages, and prosciuttos are kept.

Small Pizzas
PIZZETTE

Meatballs with Vegetables
POLPETTINE DI CARNE E VERDURE

Vegetable Puffs
SFOGLIATINE DI VERDURE

Cheese Canapes
CROSTINI DI FORMAGGIO

Canapes with Salmon Mousse
CROSTINI DI SALMONE

Canapes with Olive Spread
CROSTINI CON PASTA D'OLIVE

Fried Stuffed Olives
OLIVE FARCITE E FRITTE

Rice Balls
SUPPLÌ DI RISO

Air-Dried Venison
BRESAOLA DI CERVO

Prosciutto and Bresaola with Melon, Figs, Grapes, and Watermelon
PROSCIUTTO E BRESAOLA CON MELONE, FICHI, UVA E ANGURIA

Villa d'Este Assorted Hors D'oeuvres: Lobster, Salmon, Caviar, and Goose Liver Pâté
ANTIPASTO VILLA D'ESTE: ASTICE, SALMONE, CAVIALE E FEGATO D'OCA

Salmon Rolls Stuffed with Crabmeat and Avocado
INVOLTINI DI SALMONE CON GRANSEOLA E AVOCADO

Mozzarella, Salmon, and Basil Roll
ROTOLO DI MOZZARELLA, SALMONE E BASILICO

Eggplant Roll Stuffed with Ricotta and Vegetables
ROTOLO DI MELANZANE CON RICOTTA E VERDURE

Stuffed Zucchini Blossoms
FIORI DI ZUCCHINA FARCITI

Cold Vegetable Flan
SFORMATO DI VERDURE

Goose Liver Escalope Flavored with Balsamic Vinegar
SCALOPPE DI FEGATO D'OCA ALL'ACETO BALSAMICO

Star of Mixed Shellfish
FANTASIA DI CROSTACEI

Jumbo Shrimp Salad
INSALATA DI GAMBERONI

Lobster Salad
INSALATA DI ASTICE

Capon Salad
INSALATA DI CAPPONE

Veal Saltimbocca Salad
INSALATA DI SALTIMBOCCA

Guinea Hen Salad
INSALATA DI FARAONA

Grilled Mushrooms with Radicchio of Treviso
INSALATA DI PORCINI CON RADICCHIO DI TREVISO

canapes with salmon mousse

canapes with olive spread

cheese canapes

fried stuffed olives

rice balls

vegetable puffs

small pizzas

meatballs with vegetables

small **pizzas**

PIZZETTE

[YIELDS ABOUT 24 PIZZETTES]

PIZZA DOUGH
¼ ounce dry yeast
½ cup lukewarm water
½ pound flour
    pinch salt
4 tablespoons olive oil

GARNISH
    peeled fresh or canned plum
        tomatoes, diced
    mozzarella cheese, diced
    little pieces of anchovy fillets
        (one for each pizzette)
    oregano

1. Dissolve the yeast in the water; cover and set aside until foamy (approximately 10 minutes).

2. Sift the flour and salt together in a bowl and add the yeast.

3. Work the dough with your hands until smooth; shape into a ball, cover with a cloth that has been sprinkled with flour, and set aside for about 30 minutes, waiting for it to rise and double its size (depending on the room temperature).

4. Separate into 4 parts and shape each part of dough into small balls. Roll them out on a floured board until quite flat and round (2-inch diameter). Spread on a well-greased (use olive oil) baking sheet.

5. Garnish with the listed ingredients.

6. Sprinkle with oil and bake in a preheated oven at 425° for 10-15 minutes.

meatballs with vegetables

POLPETTINE DI CARNE E VERDURE

[6 SERVINGS]

2 garlic cloves, minced
  olive oil
2 ounces each of eggplant, pepper,
    and onion, finely chopped
3 ounces ground lamb
1 cup red wine
  salt and pepper, freshly ground
  Tabasco
  paprika
  flour
1 egg, beaten
  angel hair pasta, broken into
    pieces

1. Sauté garlic in olive oil and add vegetables.

2. When well cooked, add meat.

3. Proceed to cook slowly and add wine. Reduce on a high flame.

4. Add salt and pepper to taste, a few drops of Tabasco, and a pinch of paprika. Cooking time should amount to about half an hour.

5. When cool, make small balls from the mixture.

6. Roll in flour and the beaten egg, and cover the balls with the angel hair pasta.

7. Fry in olive oil.

vegetable puffs

SFOGLIATINE DI VERDURE

[6 SERVINGS]

1 pound puff pastry
1 pound julienne of vegetables:
    carrots, zucchini, eggplants,
    and peppers
  oil and butter
  salt and pepper, freshly ground
1 teaspoon fresh or dried thyme
1 egg, beaten

1. Roll out the puff pastry as thin as possible (less than ¼ inch) and cut into 2½ inch rounds. Sauté until al dente the vegetables in oil and butter and add salt, pepper, and thyme.

2. Brush each round of puff pastry with the beaten egg and place a spoonful of cooked vegetables in the center. Cover with a second round of puff pastry and press rim down with fingers. Brush each puff pastry with beaten egg; set aside for about an hour.

3. Place in a preheated oven at 400° for 10-15 minutes.

cheese canapes

CROSTINI DI FORMAGGIO

[6 SERVINGS]

5 ounces goat cheese
2 teaspoons olive oil
  salt and white pepper, freshly
    ground
  country bread
3 walnuts for garnish

1. Blend goat cheese, olive oil, and salt and pepper.

2. Toast slices of country bread and spread cheese mixture over each slice (with a pastry bag). Decorate each slice with half a walnut.

canapes with **salmon** mousse

CROSTINI DI SALMONE

[6 SERVINGS]

1 envelope gelatin
2 tablespoons lemon juice
1 thin slice onion
½ cup boiling water
1 cup mayonnaise (see Basic
    Recipes, page 134)
1 pound canned salmon, drained
    pinch paprika
1 teaspoon dill
1 small gherkin, chopped
1 cup heavy cream
1 tablespoon brandy

1. Empty gelatin into the blender, add lemon juice, slice of onion, and the boiling water. Blend at high speed.

2. Add mayonnaise, salmon, paprika, dill, and gherkin, and blend again at high speed.

3. Last, add cream and brandy.

4. Pour into a mold and refrigerate for a couple of hours.

canapes with **olive** spread

CROSTINI CON PASTA D'OLIVE

[6 SERVINGS]

3 ounces black olives (without pits)
1 garlic clove
2 anchovy fillets
½ tablespoon capers
1 tablespoon olive oil
    country bread

Blend all ingredients and spread over slices of toasted country bread.

fried stuffed **olives**

OLIVE FARCITE E FRITTE

[6 SERVINGS]

2 olives per person
    sausage
1 egg, beaten
    bread crumbs
    olive oil

1. Slice each olive spirally (as when peeling an orange), remove pit, and stuff with a bit of sausage.

2. Roll each olive into a beaten egg and then into bread crumbs, and fry in olive oil.

rice balls

SUPPLÌ DI RISO

[6 SERVINGS]

**RISOTTO WITH
PARMESAN CHEESE**

3 cups beef broth
   (see Basic Recipes, page 131)
4 tablespoons butter
1 small onion, finely chopped
1 cup Arborio rice
   salt and pepper, freshly ground
2 tablespoons Parmesan cheese,
   grated
   flour
   egg, beaten

STUFFING

mozzarella cheese, diced
meat sauce (see Basic Recipes,
   page 133)

1. Bring broth to a boil in a saucepan; reduce heat but keep at a slow boil. In another saucepan, melt 3 tablespoons butter; add chopped onion and cook over moderate heat, stirring constantly with a wooden spoon until the onion has turned a golden color. Add rice and stir for about 3 minutes so that every grain is coated with butter. Season with a little salt and pepper.

2. Begin adding one cup of boiling broth and continue stirring until the liquid is absorbed. Continue adding to the rice one cup at a time. It will take about 20 minutes for the rice to absorb all the broth and to finish cooking. When done, it will be tender and creamy but not soft or mushy.

3. Remove pan from heat and stir in the remaining tablespoon of butter and the grated Parmesan cheese. When the risotto has cooled, take a handful of risotto and shape it like a pear (as in photo on page 21). Fill the center with some mozzarella and meat sauce. Then roll the pear-shaped rice ball in flour and beaten egg and fry.

air-dried venison

BRESAOLA DI CERVO

[1 SERVING]

3-4 ounces thin machine-sliced
   bresaola
   extra-virgin olive oil
   juice of half lemon
   black pepper, freshly ground
   parsley, minced

1. Once the bresaola has been sliced, it should be eaten immediately; otherwise, it will dry out.

2. Arrange slices on a dish, cover with oil to moisten, add lemon juice and a dash of pepper.

3. Sprinkle with parsley.

• Bresaola is one of the most delicious antipasti. Typical of the Lombardy (Valtellina) area, it is always listed on the Villa d'Este menu. Now available throughout Italy, it is beginning to become known abroad.

prosciutto and bresaola with melon, figs, grapes, and watermelon

PROSCIUTTO E BRESAOLA CON MELONE, FICHI, UVA E ANGURIA

Arrange various ingredients as in photo. This dish can also be served as a first course or for a light summer meal.

[1 SERVING]

3 or 4 servings of Parma prosciutto
3 or 4 slices of bresaola melon
    shaped into small balls
    watermelon slice shaped
    like a leaf
    fresh figs
    grapes
    lettuce leaves

• The famous prosciutto (crudo) di Parma is now available in the United States.

villa d'este assorted hors d'oeuvres:
lobster, salmon, caviar, and goose liver pâté

ANTIPASTO VILLA D'ESTE: ASTICE, SALMONE, CAVIALE E FEGATO D'OCA

[6 SERVINGS]

3 live lobsters (weighing
   approximately 1 pound each)
½ pound goose liver pâté (below)
   court bouillon (see Basic
   Recipes, page 132)

PÂTÉ (FOR 12 PEOPLE)

1 pound goose liver
1 tablespoon each of cognac,
   sherry, and port
   salt and white pepper,
   freshly ground

GARNISH

½ pound smoked salmon
2 ounces caviar
   lettuce
   papaya
   mango
   red currants

LOBSTER

1. Boil lobsters in court bouillon for 10 minutes.

2. Cut lobsters in half lengthwise, remove meat from shell, and slice.

PÂTÉ

1. Cut open liver and remove "veins." Marinate for about 24 hours in the cognac, sherry, and port, salt, and white pepper.

2. Line a mold with grease-proof paper, press liver in, and cover with aluminum foil. Cook in a double boiler in the oven for 30-40 minutes at 225°.

3. Cool for 6-8 hours in refrigerator. Arrange on a plate, as in photo, and garnish with smoked salmon, caviar, lettuce, papaya, mango, and red currants.

salmon rolls stuffed
with crabmeat and avocado

INVOLTINI DI SALMONE CON GRANSEOLA E AVOCADO

[6 SERVINGS]

2 pounds boned and cleaned fresh
   wild salmon (do not remove skin)
3 tablespoons salt
   pepper, freshly ground
1 teaspoon sugar
   juice of 1 lemon and 1 orange
   dill

STUFFING

6 ounces cooked crabmeat
6 ounces avocado, diced and
   seasoned with oil, lemon, salt,
   and pepper

DILL SAUCE

1 cup yogurt
   mayonnaise of 1 egg (see Basic
   Recipes, page 134)
   dill

GARNISH

caviar
papaya
mango
avocado
lettuce leaves
white truffle

1. Marinate the salmon for 24 hours with the salt and pepper, sugar, lemon and orange juice, and dill.

2. Occasionally, collect juice and sprinkle over salmon.

3. Slice salmon thinly, and use 3 slices per person.

4. Spread crabmeat and diced avocado over the salmon slices and roll up.

5. Prepare the dill sauce, blending yogurt with mayonnaise and dill.

6. Spread the sauce on one side of plate and arrange salmon rolls on top. Add a sprinkling of caviar over salmon rolls and garnish with papaya, mango, avocado, lettuce leaves, a shaving of white truffle, and dill.

mozzarella, **salmon,** and **basil** roll

ROTOLO DI MOZZARELLA, SALMONE E BASILICO

[6 SERVINGS]

14 ounces mozzarella cheese
    hot water
    milk
 7 ounces smoked salmon
20 basil leaves
    tomato sauce (see Basic Recipes,
      page 132)

GARNISH
red and yellow peppers
carrot

1. Dice mozzarella and place in a double boiler, adding hot water and milk to cover, which will be discarded after the cheese has softened; then spread mozzarella out on a sheet of plastic wrap.

2. Cover immediately with salmon and basil. Roll up tightly, and tie both ends of plastic wrap. Cool in refrigerator.

3. Cut roll into slices, and decorate as in photo with peppers and carrot julienne in the center. Surround with a dash of tomato sauce.

• Prosciutto can be substituted for salmon.

eggplant **roll** stuffed
with **ricotta** and **vegetables**

ROTOLO DI MELANZANE CON RICOTTA E VERDURE

[6 SERVINGS]

- salt
- 18 slices eggplant
- 5 ounces zucchini, carrots, string beans, broccoli, etc., diced
- olive oil
- 1 egg yolk
- 1 tablespoon Parmesan cheese
- 10 ounces ricotta cheese

BASIL SAUCE

- 30 leaves basil
- 1 tablespoon olive oil
- 10 tablespoons cream
- salt and pepper, freshly ground

GARNISH

- 6 plum tomatoes
- olive oil
- salt and pepper, freshly ground
- 1 tablespoon fresh basil, finely chopped

1. Salt eggplant slices and place under a weight to remove water (for 2-3 hours); dry with paper towels and grill.

2. In the meantime, sauté the diced vegetables in a little oil. When cool, add egg yolk and Parmesan cheese and mix together with ricotta cheese.

3. Place 2 tablespoons of the ricotta and vegetable mixture on each eggplant slice, wrapping the eggplant around the mixture, and steam for about 10 minutes.

4. While the eggplant is steaming, make the basil sauce by mixing all of the ingredients in a blender.

5. Parboil tomatoes, peel, slice lengthwise, and discard seeds.

6. Marinate the tomatoes in a little olive oil, salt, pepper, and basil for an hour.

7. For each serving, arrange 3 eggplant rolls over a plate covered with basil sauce. Garnish with the marinated tomatoes.

stuffed **zucchini** blossoms

FIORI DI ZUCCHINA FARCITI

[6 SERVINGS]

  1 pound mushrooms (champignons)
  1 tablespoon olive oil
    juice of half lemon
3½ ounces cooked chicken breast,
    diced
  2 slices white bread, soaked in
    hot milk
  2 egg whites, beaten
  1 ounce each of zucchini, carrots,
    and celery, diced and sautéed
3½ ounces cream
 12 zucchini blossoms

SAUCE
  6 tablespoons cream
  2 ounces butter

GARNISH
    rucola and Trevisana lettuce
    marinated tomatoes (see Basic
    Recipes, page 133)
    shaving of truffle

1. Clean mushrooms and sauté with oil and lemon. Remove mushrooms and keep liquid.

2. Blend chicken, mushrooms, well-strained bread, 2 beaten egg whites, and sautéd vegetables. Add cream.

3. Stuff zucchini blossoms with the above and steam for about 10 minutes.

4. For the sauce, use mushroom liquid and cream. Reduce and add butter. Cut into small pieces to bind.

5. Garnish with rucola, Trevisana lettuce, diced marinated tomatoes, and truffle.

cold vegetable flan

SFORMATO DI VERDURE

[6 SERVINGS]

½ pound carrots
½ pound zucchini
½ ounces gelatin strips (isinglass)
½ pound mushrooms (champignons)
2 cups cream
¼ teaspoon of bouillon cube

SAUCE

2 pounds tomatoes
2½ tablespoons olive oil
salt and pepper, freshly ground

GARNISH

12 small carrots
12 small zucchini
12 stalks asparagus
2 or 3 plum tomatoes
6 small bunches basil

1. Boil the carrots and zucchini separately. In the meantime, soak the gelatin sheets in cold water for about 10 minutes.

2. Blend the carrots with ⅓ of the gelatin. Then blend the zucchini with another ⅓ of the gelatin and set both vegetables aside while preparing the mushrooms.

3. Cut up the mushrooms and cook with half a cup of cream and ¼ teaspoon of a bouillon cube (to add flavor). Add the remaining ⅓ of the gelatin to the mushrooms and blend. Beat the remaining 1½ cups of cream, and add ⅓ of this whipped cream to each of the vegetables and the mushrooms.

4. Fill 6 molds with the vegetables in layers: first the mushrooms, second the zucchini, and third the carrots; store in the refrigerator.

5. Puree the 2 pounds of tomatoes together with olive oil, salt, and pepper; spread on each dish.

6. Steam the carrots, zucchini, and asparagus, which are to be used for garnish.

7. Parboil the plum tomatoes and remove the skin, seeds, and liquid and dice. These are also used for decoration on top of the vegetable flan, together with basil.

goose **liver** escalope
flavored with **balsamic** vinegar

SCALOPPE DI FEGATO D'OCA ALL'ACETO BALSAMICO

1. Cut 3 slices of goose liver and sauté quickly in a well-heated nonstick pan.

[1 SERVING]

3½ ounces goose liver
 3 teaspoons balsamic vinegar
½ teaspoon salt
¼ apple
½ teaspoon honey
 choice of salad greens

GARNISH
carrot, shredded
celery
olive oil and vinegar
salt and pepper, freshly ground

2. Remove liver and fat; add the balsamic vinegar to the pan. Reduce and add salt. Set juice aside.

3. Peel the ¼ apple, slice it, and cover with the honey. Then place under broiler.

4. Season the shredded carrots and celery with oil and vinegar, salt and pepper; place the 3 slices of goose liver on the plate, top with the sauce of balsamic vinegar, and add the apple, as in the photo.

star of mixed shellfish

FANTASIA DI CROSTACEI

[1 SERVING]

court bouillon (see Basic Recipes,
 page 132)
1½ ounces small shrimp
6 medium shrimp
4 jumbo shrimp
 half lobster
1½ ounces crabmeat

GARNISH
chopped salad greens
radish and chives

1. Cook separately in court bouillon:
small shrimp, 1 minute
medium shrimp, 2 minutes
jumbo shrimp, 3 minutes
lobster, 10 minutes
crabmeat, 15 minutes

2. Arrange shellfish as in photo, atop chopped salad greens. In the center, place a radish and chives.

jumbo shrimp salad

INSALATA DI GAMBERONI

1. Sauté vegetables in oil with garlic, sage, rosemary, and bay leaf. Pour in vinegar; reduce. Add wine and reduce. Cook for 35-40 minutes. If necessary, add tablespoon of court bouillon.

2. Cool and blend after removing garlic and bay leaf. Add mayonnaise; whisk.

3. Boil separately zucchini, carrots, and potatoes cut in rounds.

4. Display the shrimp over the bed of vegetables and mayonnaise sauce. Use zucchini, carrots, and potatoes for garnish.

[6 SERVINGS]

6 or 7 jumbo shrimp per person,
   cooked in court bouillon (see
   Basic Recipes, page 132) for
   less than 5 minutes
2 ounces each of celery, carrot,
   and onion, chopped
   olive oil
   garlic, sage, rosemary, and
   bay leaf
1 tablespoon red wine vinegar
1 cup white wine
6 tablespoons mayonnaise (see
   Basic Recipes, page 134) with
   Worcestershire sauce and
   Tabasco (a few drops of each)

GARNISH

2 ounces each of zucchini,
   carrots, and potatoes

lobster salad

INSALATA DI ASTICE

[6 SERVINGS]

3 lobsters (1½ pounds each;
   1 lobster for 2 people)
   court bouillon
      (see Basic Recipes, page 132)

YOGURT SAUCE
blend together:
2 cups lowfat yogurt
   juice of ½ grapefruit
3 walnuts, halved

GARNISH
1 avocado
1 grapefruit
   chives
3 walnuts

1. Cook lobsters in court bouillon for 20 minutes. Slice each lobster in half lengthwise.

2. Garnish the sliced lobsters with slices of avocado, grapefruit, and chives.

3. Place the yogurt sauce in the center of the plate, with a halved walnut on top.

capon salad

INSALATA DI CAPPONE

[6 SERVINGS]

1 yellow and 1 red pepper, roasted
1 small capon (3-4 pounds)
2 zucchini
2 carrots
3½ ounces string beans, cooked
1 medium eggplant, peeled,
    cut up and sautéed
5 ounces "Mostarda di Cremona"
    (sweet and sour candied fruit)
1 teaspoon dry mustard
    salt and pepper, freshly ground

GARNISH

3½ ounces shredded Parmesan
    cheese

1. Roast the peppers in the oven or on the stovetop over a high flame. Continue turning peppers over until they become completely black. When cool enough to handle, remove outer blackened skin, which will peel off. Then remove the cap and seeds by rinsing under cold water. Shred lengthwise into strips and set aside.

2. Boil capon with zucchini and carrots until capon is cooked.

3. Remove the vegetables and set aside. Remove the capon.

4. When the capon has cooled, remove the meat from carcass and shred.

5. Steep the capon, zucchini, carrots, string beans, and eggplant in the juice of the Mostarda di Cremona, the dry mustard, and the Mostarda di Cremona fruits (chopped) for 7-8 hours.

6. Add salt and pepper to taste.

7. Prepare plate with the vegetables underneath, the capon and Parmesan cheese on top. Place under broiler before serving. The additional Cremona mustard fruits are for decoration.

veal **saltimbocca** salad

INSALATA DI SALTIMBOCCA

[6 SERVINGS]

24 sage leaves
 6 slices prosciutto crudo
   (each slice divided by 4)
 1 pound veal (4 slices per person)
   olive oil
 1 cup white wine
 1 tablespoon butter
   choice of salad greens

GARNISH
shaving of black truffle
julienne of radishes, celery,
   carrots, red and yellow
   peppers, and diced tomatoes

1. Place 1 sage leaf and slice of prosciutto on top of each slice of veal. Sauté veal in oil on both sides (first on the prosciutto and sage side).

2. Remove fat. Add the wine; reduce.

3. Take out the veal and add butter to the pan to bind, without bringing to a boil. Use this sauce on top of the veal.

4. Prepare some mixed greens, seasoned lightly to taste. Arrange as in photo: the veal over the greens, topped with the truffle and the julienne of raw vegetables as a garnish.

guinea hen salad

INSALATA DI FARAONA

[6 SERVINGS]

4 half guinea hen breasts
  olive oil
  salt and pepper, freshly ground
1 cup Marsala wine
1 tablespoon butter
1 pound rucola
  olive oil and vinegar

GARNISH
½ pound bacon
5 slices toasted bread, diced
  tomato, sliced

1. Sauté the breasts in oil with salt and pepper. Remove meat and fat.

2. Add Marsala wine; reduce. Last, add the butter to bind. Set aside.

3. Julienne the bacon and sauté; then add the diced bread for the croutons. Place the fowl slices on top of seasoned rucola. Cover with Marsala sauce.

4. Garnish with croutons, bacon, and the tomato.

grilled mushrooms
with radicchio of treviso

INSALATA DI PORCINI CON RADICCHIO DI TREVISO

[6 SERVINGS]

porcini mushrooms
   (about 3 per person)
olive oil
1 clove garlic, unpeeled
  salt and pepper, freshly ground
  radicchio di Treviso salad
  balsamic vinegar
  fresh herbs (optional)
  tomatoes, sliced (optional)
  corn (optional)

1. Clean mushrooms and grill them.

2. In a saucepan, sauté mushrooms in oil with unpeeled garlic, salt, and pepper.

3. Discard garlic.

4. Arrange salad as in photo, with mushrooms in the center. Sprinkle with oil, balsamic vinegar, salt, and pepper.

5. Decorate by adding fresh herbs, tomato slices, and corn (optional).

PRIMI

In the photo is
Luciano Parolari, our executive
chef, in the main kitchen of the
hotel, making cannelloni and various types of fresh pasta.

first courses

Tortellini in Broth
TORTELLINI IN BRODO

Fish Soup
ZUPPA DI PESCE

Vegetable Soup with Pesto
MINESTRONE CON PESTO

Pasta and Beans
PASTA E FAGIOLI

Ricotta and Spinach Gnocchi
GNOCCHI DI RICOTTA E SPINACI

Potato and Vegetable Gnocchetti in a Cheese Basket
GNOCCHETTI DI VERDURE E PATATE IN CROSTA DI FORMAGGIO

Semolina and Mushroom Gnocchi
GNOCCHI DI SEMOLINO E FUNGHI

Florentine Gnocchi Roll
RULLO DI GNOCCHI ALLA FIORENTINA

Pappardelle with Rabbit Sauce
PAPPARDELLE CON SUGO DI LEPRE

Pasta Packet Stuffed with Vegetables and Ricotta
FAGOTTINO DI PASTA CON VERDURE E RICOTTA

Green Pasta Packet Stuffed with Seafood
FAGOTTINO VERDE DI FRUTTI DI MARE

Cannelloni Villa d'Este
CANNELLONI VILLA D'ESTE

Black and White Tortelloni Stuffed with Fish
TORTELLONI BIANCHI E NERI CON PESCE

Cappelloni of Mascarpone and Walnuts
CAPPELLONI DI MASCARPONE E NOCI

Half Moons of Vegetables with Sweet Peppers and Tomato Sauce
MEZZELUNE DI VERDURE CON SALSA DI PEPERONE DOLCE E POMODORO

White and Green Thin Noodles with Meat Sauce
TAGLIOLINI BIANCHI E VERDI CON SALSA BOLOGNESE

Noodles with Fondue and White Truffle
FETTUCCINE CON FONDUTA E TARTUFI BIANCHI

Black Noodles with Smoked Salmon
FETTUCCINE NERE CON SALMONE

Green Lasagnette with Fish
LASAGNETTE VERDI CON PESCE

Vegetable Lasagnette
LASAGNETTE DI VERDURE

Spinach and Ricotta Crepes
CRESPELLE DI RICOTTA E SPINACI

Spaghetti with Seafood
SPAGHETTI CON FRUTTI DI MARE

Penne with Vegetables
PENNE CON VERDURE

Orecchiette with Broccoli
ORECCHIETTE CON BROCCOLO

Risotto with Spring Vegetables
RISOTTO PRIMAVERA

Black Squid Ink Risotto
RISOTTO NERO ALLE SEPPIE

Risotto with Lemon and Shrimp
RISOTTO AL LIMONE CON SCAMPI

tortellini in broth

TORTELLINI IN BRODO

[6 SERVINGS]

Homemade pasta (see Basic
Recipes, page 134)

FILLING

1½ pounds mixed ground beef and
veal
butter
4 slices prosciutto crudo, shredded
2 mortadella slices, finely chopped
½ cup Parmesan cheese, grated
1 egg
nutmeg, freshly ground
salt
pepper, freshly ground
capon or chicken broth (see
Basic Recipes, page 131):
2 cups per person

GARNISH

green peas
tomatoes: parboiled, peeled,
seeded, and diced
Parmesan cheese, grated

1. Cut the sheets of homemade pasta into discs (2-inch diameter).

2. Sauté the ground meat in a little butter. When cooked, mix with the prosciutto, mortadella, Parmesan cheese, and egg, and season with nutmeg, salt, and pepper.

3. Blend in a food processor.

4. Place a little less than a teaspoon of filling in the center of each disc, double over the pasta after moistening the edges with water, and form a half moon, without having the edges meet.

5. Bring broth to a boil and drop in tortellini (about 14 per person). If well dried, they will take about 10 minutes to cook. If freshly made, tortellini can cook in even less than 5 minutes. Taste for firmness.

6. Add boiled green peas and diced tomatoes. Serve with grated Parmesan cheese.

fish soup

ZUPPA DI PESCE

[6 SERVINGS]

3 pounds of fish: turbot, monkfish,
    rascasse (known as scorfano in
    Italy; used only in fish soups)
1 pound lobster
    pinch of saffron
12 clams
12 mussels
3 tablespoons olive oil
2 cloves garlic
1 medium onion, chopped
1 medium carrot, chopped
2 stalks celery, chopped
1 leek, chopped
1 fennel, sliced lengthwise
6 shrimp
1 cup white wine
    country bread
    garlic
    extra-virgin olive oil

1. Clean all the fish and slice into fillets.

2. Prepare a fish stock with all the fish leftovers (see Basic Recipes, page 131). Add the lobster. Remove the lobster after 15 minutes and remove meat from shell.

3. The fish stock should simmer for at least 20 minutes. Skim; then add saffron.

4. Clean clams and mussels, and sauté in oil in a nonstick pan until they open.

5. Discard those that have not opened up. Remove clams and mussels from their shells. Save the liquid; filter and add it to the fish stock.

6. In a large pot, sauté in olive oil the garlic, onion, carrot, celery, leek, and fennel.

7. Add the fillets of turbot, monkfish, and rascasse, the lobster, shrimp, clams, and mussels.

8. Add a cup of white wine; reduce. Add the fish stock. Simmer for about 15 minutes.

9. For each serving, rub 2 slices of toasted country bread with garlic, and brush them with oil. Add soup and serve.

vegetable **soup** with **pesto**

MINESTRONE CON PESTO

[6 SERVINGS]

2–3 tablespoons olive oil
¼ cup salt pork, diced
1 leek
1 celery stalk
2 carrots
2 zucchini
½ cup string beans, chopped
2 cups cabbage, shredded
2 medium potatoes, cut up
2 tomatoes, diced
1 bay leaf
½ cup beans (canned cannellini)
½ cup green peas
salt
Parmesan cheese, grated

PESTO

2 cups fresh basil leaves
1½ cups good olive oil, preferably produced in the Liguria region
½ cup pine nuts
¾ cup Parmesan cheese, grated
1 teaspoon coarse salt
¾ teaspoon garlic, chopped

1. Add olive oil to a 7-quart pot, and sauté salt pork.

2. Begin adding all the ingredients in the order listed, cooking each vegetable for 2–3 minutes before adding another. (If you like to plan ahead, prepare all your ingredients as directed and add everything at the same time. In either case, the vegetables are to be served with water and seasoned. Naturally, if using canned vegetables, they should be added only minutes before the soup is ready.)

3. Cover and simmer for 2 hours.

4. Prepare pesto by combining all ingredients in a food processor.

5. Add 2 tablespoons of pesto to the center of each bowl. Serve with Parmesan cheese.

• Minestrone can be served hot or cold and can be kept for several days.
• A rind of Parmesan cheese will add flavor, but should be removed when the soup is cooked.
• Instead of pesto, a tablespoon of Tuscan olive oil can be poured on top of each soup portion upon serving.

pasta and beans

PASTA E FAGIOLI

[6 SERVINGS]

½ pound dried borlotti beans
1 bay leaf
1 garlic clove
  about 6 fresh sage leaves
5 tablespoons olive oil
2 ounces pancetta (salt pork),
  chopped
2 celery stalks, chopped
2 medium onions, chopped
2 medium carrots, chopped
6 cups water
¼ pound fresh tagliatelle (see
  Basic Recipes, page 134)
1 tablespoon fresh thyme
1 tablespoon fresh rosemary
  sprigs, finely chopped
  salt
  pepper, freshly ground

1. Soak beans in cold water overnight.

2. Drain beans, place in a casserole dish, and cover with water.

3. Place in a preheated oven at 250°F, adding bay leaf, garlic, sage, and 1 tablespoon olive oil. Cover and bake for 1½ hours.

4. Sauté in a large saucepan pancetta, celery, onions, and carrots in 4 heated tablespoons of oil.

5. Pour in 6 cups water, reduce heat, and simmer for 1 hour.

6. In the meantime, purée half the beans (without the sage and bay leaf), and add these and the whole beans with their liquid to the saucepan. Bring to a boil; add the tagliatelle. When cooked, sprinkle in the thyme and rosemary; salt and pepper to taste.

7. A teaspoon of olive oil can be poured over each portion.

• Tagliatelle is a variety of pasta that is similar to fettucine, but at ¼-inch wide, not quite as narrow.

46

ricotta and spinach gnocchi

GNOCCHI DI RICOTTA E SPINACI

[6 SERVINGS]

6 ounces spinach, cooked
  olive oil
1 garlic clove
1 pound ricotta cheese
2 eggs
2 ounces Parmesan cheese,
  freshly grated
  nutmeg, freshly ground
  salt
  pepper, freshly ground
1 tablespoon butter
1 tablespoon basil, chopped
3 cups tomato sauce (see Basic
  Recipes, page 132)
6 tomatoes (optional)

1. Sauté the spinach in oil with garlic (discard garlic when spinach is cooked). When cool, blend.

2. Add ricotta cheese, eggs, Parmesan, and nutmeg.

3. Salt and pepper to taste.

4. Shape with a spoon, as in photo, and steam for 6–7 minutes.

5. Combine butter and chopped basil and blend together with tomato sauce. Heat and spread on plate.

6. Arrange gnocchi as above and decorate in the center with a tomato shaped into a flower.

potato and vegetable gnocchetti in a cheese basket

GNOCCHETTI DI VERDURE E PATATE IN CROSTA DI FORMAGGIO

1. Boil potatoes, peel, and mash. Cool and spread out on a marble surface. Add flour, Parmesan, egg yolk, salt, and nutmeg.

[6 SERVINGS]

WHITE GNOCCHETTI
10½ ounces potatoes
3½ ounces flour
1 tablespoon Parmesan cheese, grated
1 egg yolk
salt
nutmeg, freshly ground

2. Mix together without kneading and shape by hand into gnocchetti.

3. Cook in boiling salted water until they surface. To make the green and red gnocchetti, use the same procedure as above.

GREEN GNOCCHETTI
1½ pounds potatoes
3½ ounces cooked spinach, chopped
finely and strained well
1 tablespoon Parmesan cheese, grated
1 egg yolk
salt
nutmeg, freshly ground

4. To make the baskets, melt cheese in a nonstick pan and quickly turn upside-down over a cup and let cheese cool.

5. Sauté all the gnocchetti in butter and sage and place in the baskets.

RED GNOCCHETTI
1½ pounds potatoes
3½ ounces beets, finely chopped
1 tablespoon Parmesan cheese, grated
1 egg yolk
salt
nutmeg, freshly ground

butter
sage
½ cup diced hard cheese per basket

• These gnocchetti can also be used as a side dish with any kind of meat.

48

semolina and mushroom gnocchi

GNOCCHI DI SEMOLINO E FUNGHI

[6 SERVINGS]

1½ pounds porcini mushrooms (or
    champignons)
    olive oil
  5 cups milk
    nutmeg, freshly ground
    salt
  2 tablespoons butter
1½ cups Italian semolina
  4 egg yolks
 ½ cup Parmesan cheese, grated

GARNISH

  2 small zucchini, sautéed and
    sliced lengthwise
  2 tomatoes, marinated (see Basic
    Recipes, page 133)

SAUCE (optional)

12 tablespoons brown sauce (see
    Basic Recipes, page 133)

1. Sauté sliced mushrooms in a little oil. Set half aside for garnishing. Dice the rest of the mushrooms to use in the semolina gnocchi.

2. Bring to a boil the milk together with nutmeg, salt, and butter; lower heat and pour in the semolina in a steady stream, stirring until it becomes a thick mixture in which a wooden spoon will stand up. This should take a total of 20–25 minutes.

3. Remove from heat and stir in egg yolks and Parmesan cheese. Last, add the diced mushrooms.

4. Oil a Formica counter, pour the mixture on the surface and flatten it out. Allow it to cool. Cut the semolina mixture into discs about 2 inches in diameter. Arrange in an ovenproof dish, dot with butter, and place under broiler.

5. Prepare each plate individually: Overlap, as in photo, one slice mushroom (of those set aside) with one semolina gnoccho. Dice and sauté in oil the rest of the mushrooms, add the zucchini and tomatoes, and place in the center of the plate. If using brown sauce, spread it around gnocchi.

florentine gnocchi roll

RULLO DI GNOCCHI ALLA FIORENTINA

[6 SERVINGS]

1 pound potatoes
1½ cups all-purpose flour
4 tablespoons Parmesan cheese,
   grated
5 egg yolks
   salt and pepper, freshly ground
½ pound spinach
   butter and 1 additional
      tablespoon Parmesan
   tomato sauce (see Basic Recipes,
      page 132)

1. Steam potatoes to retain flavor; peel and pass through a ricer and mix with flour, Parmesan, egg yolks, salt, and pepper.

2. Knead slightly and shape dough into a square.

3. Place on napkin and spread the spinach, previously sautéed in butter, over the dough.

4. Roll it up inside the napkin; then tie up with string, like sausage.

5. Boil it for 40 minutes.

6. After removing the napkin, slice the roll.

7. On each disk consisting of 2 or 3 slices, add a little tomato sauce, a sprinkling of Parmesan, and a little melted butter.

pappardelle with rabbit sauce

PAPPARDELLE CON SUGO DI LEPRE

[6 SERVINGS]

10½ ounces all-purpose flour
10½ ounces buckwheat flour
6 eggs
1 tablespoon olive oil
pinch of salt

RABBIT SAUCE

1 small rabbit
1 bottle red wine
1 cup red vinegar
onion, carrot, and celery, coarsely chopped
rosemary, garlic, parsley, cloves, juniper berries, cinnamon, bay leaf
½ cup mushrooms that have been soaked in water and strained olive oil

1. Following the procedure for homemade pasta (see Basic Recipes, page 134), prepare pappardelle using ingredients at left. Pappardelle are similar to noodles, only wider (from ½ to 1 inch) and irregular in length.

2. Cut the rabbit into pieces and marinate overnight in the wine and with all the listed ingredients for the sauce.

3. Remove meat and set aside.

4. Remove vegetables from wine and sauté them in 1 tablespoon of oil; then add rabbit and wine. Cook.

5. Remove meat from bones. Blend vegetables with the juices.

6. Heat together rabbit and vegetable sauce and pour over the cooked pappardelle.

pasta packet **stuffed** with **vegetables** and **ricotta**

FAGOTTINO DI PASTA CON VERDURE E RICOTTA

[6 SERVINGS]

1 6x6 square of homemade
  pasta per person (see Basic
  Recipes, page 134)

STUFFING

1 pound diced vegetables (zucchini,
  eggplant, carrots, radicchio,
  celery, etc.), sautéed in butter
1 pound ricotta cheese
3 eggs
1 tablespoon Parmesan cheese,
  grated
6 strips of leek

SAUCE

12 tablespoons tomato sauce (see
   Basic Recipes, page 132)
6 tablespoons cream

1. Mix vegetables with ricotta cheese, eggs, and the Parmesan.

2. Cook pasta in boiling water. Drain.

3. Place the vegetable mixture in the center of each square. Pick up the four corners and tie them together with a strip of parboiled leek.

4. Steam "fagottini" for 5–6 minutes.

5. Blend the tomato sauce with the cream.

6. Spread the sauce on each plate. Place the fagottino in the center.

7. With a toothpick, make a design on the sauce, similar to sun rays.

green **pasta** packet
stuffed with **seafood**

FAGOTTINO VERDE DI FRUTTI DI MARE

[6 SERVINGS]

1 6x6 square of homemade pasta
    per person (see Basic Recipes,
    page 134, for green pasta)
6 strips of leeks

STUFFING

½ pounds each: sea bass, salmon,
    scallops, shrimp
    olive oil
1 garlic clove
    grappa
2 tablespoons marinated tomatoes
    (see Basic Recipes, page 133)

SAUCE

2 cups white sauce (see Basic
    Recipes, page 132)
    saffron

1. Sauté fish in oil with garlic.

2. Remove garlic and cook briefly with grappa.

3. Add marinated tomatoes and cook for 5–6 minutes. Divide mixture in half: the first half is for stuffing; the other half for garnishing.

4. Add to second half of fish the white sauce and a pinch of saffron.

5. Cook pasta in boiling water. Drain.

6. Place the fish mixture in the center of each square. Pick up the four corners and tie them together with a strip of parboiled leek.

7. Steam the fagottini for 5–6 minutes.

8. Spread the sauce on each plate and place the fagottino in the center. With a little tomato sauce, create a design as in photo, and surround each fagottino with the variety of fish set aside.

cannelloni **villa d'este**

CANNELLONI VILLA D'ESTE

[6 SERVINGS]

homemade pasta (see Basic
   Recipes, page 134)
2 ounces spinach, cooked,
   strained, and finely chopped

STUFFING

2 ounces each of carrot, onion,
   celery, chopped
olive oil
5 ounces each of veal, beef, and
   pork, ground
1 cup white wine
3½ ounces mushrooms
   (champignons)
1½ ounces sweetbreads
   carrot, onion, celery stalk
2 ounces cooked chicken breasts
1 egg
2 ounces Parmesan cheese, grated

SAUCE

Mix 1 tablespoon tomato sauce
   (see Basic Recipes, page 132)
   with 6 tablespoons cream

GARNISH

tomato, sliced
basil leaves

1. Before kneading, remove one quarter of the dough to make the green pasta by adding spinach. Roll out the big ball of dough into 4 x 3 rectangular sheets, and cut the green dough into fettuccine.

2. Place green fettuccine over white pasta sheets and pass through a pasta machine.

3. Sauté the chopped vegetables in oil. Add meat and wine; reduce. Continue to cook slowly for 40 minutes. Blend.

4. Cook mushrooms and sweetbreads separately. Slice mushrooms and sauté them in a little oil.

5. The sweetbreads should be left under running water for a couple of hours, then boiled for 20 minutes with carrot, onion, and celery. Remove membrane and dice.

6. Add mushrooms and sweetbreads to meat stuffing.

7. Dice chicken and mix together with egg and Parmesan cheese. Combine with the stuffing.

8. Place a small rectangular stuffing mixture in the center of each cannelloni. Wrap up and twist the ends, as in photo. Cook cannelloni in boiling salted water.

9. Spread tomato and cream sauce on each plate. Place cannelloni (3 per person) on top, and garnish with sliced tomato and basil leaves.

black and white tortelloni stuffed with sea food

TORTELLONI BIANCHI E NERI CON PESCE

[6 SERVINGS]

BLACK PASTA
1 tablespoon onion, chopped
1 tablespoon olive oil
2½ ounces ink squid
¼ cup white wine
1⅓ cups all-purpose flour
2 egg yolks

WHITE PASTA
1 cup all-purpose flour
1 egg
1 teaspoon olive oil

FISH STUFFING
1 small shallot, chopped
2 tablespoons olive oil
1 garlic clove
1 pound fish (sole, turbot, etc.),
   cut into small pieces
   rosemary and thyme
   crabmeat and lobster, cooked
½ cup white wine
   salt and pepper, freshly ground
1 slice white bread
1 egg

SAUCE
1 cup fish stock (broth)
1 cup cream
2 cups tomato sauce (see Basic
   Recipes, page 132)
1 teaspoon butter

1. Sauté onion in oil. Add squid with its ink; pour in wine and cook about 5–6 minutes, until liquid is reduced. When cool, in a food processor mix the ink squeezed out from the ink sacs, chopped squid, flour and egg yolks.

2. Process the white pasta separately. Run both black and white dough separately through a pasta machine.

3. Stretch out the black and white sheets of dough, letting them rest while you prepare the fish stuffing. Sauté shallot in oil with garlic. Remove garlic and add fish, rosemary, and thyme.

4. Pour in the wine, salt, and pepper. Cook for a few minutes, until wine is reduced. Save some of the fish for garnish. Put through a food processor together with the crumbled slice of bread and the whole egg.

5. Cut each sheet of dough into two. Place 1 teaspoon of fish filling on one sheet (previously brushed with a lightly beaten egg) about 2 inches apart from the next teaspoon of filling. Place second sheet over the first and press around each mound of filling. Cut each tortelloni with a fluted pastry wheel into circles about 2½ inches in diameter. Bring to a boil a very large saucepan of water and cook the tortelloni.

SAUCE
Reduce the fish stock. Add cream; reduce again and add tomato sauce. Simmer for a few minutes and add butter to bind. Arrange sauce and tortelloni as in photo, and garnish with the reserved fish, diced tomato, and a few sprigs of parsley.

cappelloni of mascarpone and walnuts

CAPPELLONI DI MASCARPONE E NOCI

[6 SERVINGS]

homemade pasta (see Basic
Recipes, page 134)

STUFFING

10½ ounces mascarpone
2 egg yolks
2 ounces Parmesan cheese,
grated
salt
pepper, freshly ground
nutmeg, freshly ground
6 walnuts, finely chopped

GARNISH

1 pound julienne of carrots,
zucchini, and leeks sautéed
in butter and oil
2 tablespoons mascarpone
walnuts
diced tomatoes (optional)

SAUCE

½ cup butter
5 tablespoons Parmesan cheese,
grated

1. Cut sheets of homemade pasta into discs (3½ inches in diameter) with a fluted pastry wheel.

2. Prepare the stuffing, combining all the listed ingredients.

3. Place a tablespoon of stuffing in the center of each disc; after moistening the edges with water, double over the pasta, making sure the edges do not meet. Wrap around your index finger, and with your thumb press edges together.

4. Turn over one edge to form a peak, as in photo.

5. Cook cappelloni in boiling salted water and drain.

6. Place 4 cappelloni on each dish over a bed of vegetables.

7. Place julienned vegetables on plate. Heat butter and whisk with Parmesan. Pour over the cappelloni; top with mascarpone.

8. Garnish in the center with walnuts and a sprinkling of diced tomatoes.

half-moons of vegetables with sweet peppers and tomato sauce

MEZZELUNE DI VERDURE CON SALSA DI PEPERONE DOLCE E POMODORO

[6 SERVINGS]

homemade pasta (see Basic
   Recipes, page 134)
4 ounces spinach, cooked,
   strained, and finely chopped

STUFFING

1 ounce Ricotta cheese
2 tablespoons Parmesan cheese,
   grated
1 egg yolk
3 ounces carrots, zucchini, and
   leeks, diced and sautéed in oil
   and butter

SAUCE

1 small onion, chopped
1 red and 1 yellow pepper,
   parboiled and chopped
4 plum tomatoes, parboiled,
   peeled, seeded, and diced
   olive oil
1 cup beef broth (see Basic
   Recipes, page 131)
½ teaspoon of salt
1 bay leaf
1 tablespoon butter

1. Before kneading, remove half the dough to make green pasta by adding spinach.

2. Prepare the stuffing by combining all the listed ingredients.

3. Cut up the pasta sheets into discs (2½ inches in diameter) with a fluted pastry wheel. Place 1 teaspoon of stuffing in the center of each disc, double up disc and press edges together.

4. Sauté onion, peppers, and tomatoes in oil.

5. Add broth, salt, and bay leaf. When cooked, remove bay leaf. Blend and add butter to bind.

6. Spread sauce on each plate. Place 6 half-moons (3 of green pasta and 3 of white pasta) on top and decorate with a tomato or a pepper. Ribbons of white and green fettuccine (as shown in photo) are optional.

white and green thin noodles with bolognese sauce

TAGLIOLINI BIANCHI E VERDI CON SALSA BOLOGNESE

[6 SERVINGS]

homemade pasta (see Basic
Recipes, page 134)
4 ounces spinach, cooked,
strained, and finely chopped
Bolognese (meat) sauce (see
Basic Recipes, page 133)

1. Before kneading, remove half the dough to make green pasta by adding spinach.

2. Cut up or pass through the pasta machine the white and green sheets, until as thin as possible (about half the size of the noodles).

3. Green and white pasta should be cooked separately, since the spinach pasta cooks faster.

4. Drain the green noodles first; immediately follow with the white noodles. Pour the meat sauce over the noodles and toss.

5. Serve immediately. Note: Grated Parmesan cheese can be served at the table, but Italians generally do not use Parmesan with meat sauce. The green and white pasta is also commonly known as paglia e fieno, meaning "straw and hay."

noodles with fondue and white truffle

FETTUCCINE CON FONDUTA E TARTUFI BIANCHI

[6 SERVINGS]

Noodles of homemade pasta
  (see Basic Recipes, page 134)

FONDUE
2 cups Fontina cheese, diced
1½ cups milk
1 tablespoon butter
  salt
4 egg yolks
1 tablespoon olive oil
  white truffle from Alba
  (Piedmont)

1. Steep diced cheese in milk for a couple of hours.

2. In a double boiler, melt cheese with milk on a low flame with butter and a little salt.

3. Stir until cheese is melted. Add the egg yolks, one at a time, to prevent curdling; continue beating with a wire whisk until the mixture thickens and becomes smooth and shiny.

4. Cook noodles in boiling salted water with a tablespoon of olive oil to prevent noodles from sticking together. In 2–3 minutes, the noodles will surface. Quickly drain the noodles and toss with fondue sauce.

5. Serve with a shaving of truffle on top.

black **noodles** with **smoked** salmon

FETTUCCINE NERE CON SALMONE

[6 SERVINGS]

1 tablespoon onion, chopped
1 tablespoon olive oil
5 ounces ink squid
½ cup white wine
4½ cups all-purpose flour
5 egg yolks
7 ounces julienne of smoked salmon
   butter
   vodka

1. Sauté onion in oil, add the squid with its ink, pour in wine, and cook for 5–6 minutes, until liquid is reduced.

2. When cool, mix in a food processor the ink squeezed out from the ink sacs, the chopped-up squid, the flour, and the egg yolks. Roll out the black dough and cut it into noodles.

3. In the meantime, sauté the julienne of smoked salmon in butter, and add a small amount of vodka.

4. Cook noodles in boiling salted water; drain as usual. Keep a couple of tablespoons of the water in which the noodles were cooked. Return noodles to the pan and quickly sauté with the reserved water and a tablespoon of butter.

5. Add the salmon.

6. Toss again and serve.

green **lasagnette** with **fish**

LASAGNETTE VERDI CON PESCE

[6 SERVINGS]

homemade green pasta (see
  Basic Recipes, page 134)

SAUCE

1½ pounds of various fish such as,
  turbot, shrimp, cuttlefish
  without ink sacs, clams, etc.
  olive oil
  1 garlic clove
  1 cup white wine
  6 tablespoons marinated tomatoes
  or 1 cup tomato sauce (see
  Basic Recipes, page 133)
  2 cups white sauce (see Basic
  Recipes, page 132)
  1 tablespoon fresh rosemary,
  chopped, and combined with
  1 tablespoon butter
  2 tablespoons Parmesan cheese,
  grated
  butter

1. Cut up the sheets of pasta into postcard-size rectangles. Cook the pasta in boiling salted water. Stir with a wooden spoon; as soon as the pasta surfaces, drain and rinse under cold water.

2. In the meantime, prepare the fish sauce. When all the fish has been cleaned, shelled, and cooked, sauté it in oil and garlic. Pour in wine, and evaporate by half; add the tomatoes or tomato sauce, the white sauce, and the rosemary-butter mixture.

3. Preheat oven to 400°.

4. In a slightly greased ovenproof dish, spread a little fish sauce on the bottom; add a layer of lasagna and continue filling the dish in the same order. Four layers will be sufficient.

5. Top with Parmesan cheese and dot with butter.

6. Bake for a few minutes. In the photo, the lasagna is prepared in individual portions with a garnish of fish sauce.

vegetable lasagnette

LASAGNETTE DI VERDURE

[6 SERVINGS]

homemade pasta (see Basic
  Recipes, page 134)
⅓ pound each of string beans,
  artichokes, asparagus, fennel,
  zucchini, and eggplant,
  chopped
olive oil
butter
1 tablespoon pesto (see
  Minestrone, page 45)
4 cups white sauce (see Basic
  Recipes, page 132)
2 tablespoons marinated tomatoes
  (see Basic Recipes, page 133)
3 tablespoons Parmesan cheese,
  grated

1. Prepare pasta as in previous recipe.

2. Sauté all vegetables in oil and butter; add the pesto, white sauce, and tomatoes.

3. Layer pasta and vegetable mixture.

4. Cover generously with the Parmesan cheese and dot with butter.

5. Bake in a preheated oven at 400°.

6. Recipe can be made in individual portions and decorated with vegetables, as in photo.

spinach and ricotta crepes

CRESPELLE DI RICOTTA E SPINACI

[6 SERVINGS]

6 eggs
9 ounces all-purpose flour
3 tablespoons melted butter
2 cups milk
  salt
  nutmeg, freshly ground

FILLING

Combine 10½ ounces ricotta
  cheese with 10½ ounces
  spinach, cooked, strained, and
  finely chopped

SAUCE

Blend 2 cups white sauce (see
  Basic Recipes, page 132) with
  12 basil leaves
3 tablespoons marinated tomatoes
  (see Basic Recipes, page 133)

1. Combine eggs with flour; add butter, milk, salt, and nutmeg. Beat with a whisk until smooth (batter can be refrigerated for an hour before using).

2. Make individual crepes (2–3 tablespoons batter per crepe) in a crepe pan, filmed with oil.

3. Fill each crepe with the ricotta and spinach; roll up.

4. Cover with white sauce and dot with marinated tomatoes.

5. Place under broiler until a golden crust has formed on top.

6. Serve 2 half-crepes per person.

spaghetti with seafood

SPAGHETTI CON FRUTTI DI MARE

[6 SERVINGS]

1 pound spaghetti

SAUCE

½ pound clams, unshelled
½ pound mussels, unshelled
olive oil
2 or 3 garlic cloves
½ teaspoon hot red-pepper flakes
12 shrimp
2 cuttlefish (without ink sacs)
6 scallops
4 tablespoons marinated tomatoes
(see Basic Recipes, page 133)
3 tablespoons parsley, minced

1. Scrub clams and mussels. Sauté them in a skillet with oil and garlic over a high flame until the shells open up. Discard the unopened ones.

2. Keep some clams and mussels in their shells. Save the liquid.

3. Sauté in the same pan the garlic (remove once oil is flavored) and pepper flakes. Add all fish except the clams and mussels.

4. When cooked, add the marinated tomatoes and last, clams, mussels, and parsley.

5. Cook the spaghetti in boiling salted water. Drain.

6. Add the fish sauce; toss and serve.

penne with vegetables

PENNE CON VERDURE

[6 SERVINGS]

1 pound penne
3 zucchini
1 yellow pepper
1 red pepper
2 artichokes
1 eggplant
12 asparagus stalks
   olive oil
2 cups marinated tomatoes (see
   Basic Recipes, page 133)
   Parmesan cheese (optional)

1. In a large skillet, sauté all listed vegetables (chopped or cut into strips) in olive oil. When cooked, add marinated tomatoes.

2. In the meantime, cook the penne in boiling salted water. Drain.

3. Add the penne to the skillet of vegetables; sauté for a couple of minutes. Add Parmesan cheese, if desired.

• Many variations can be made on this dish. For instance, "Penne with Zucchini" is quick and easy to prepare. While the penne (or macaroni, sedanini, etc.) are cooking in boiling salted water, dice a couple of zucchini and add them to the pasta about 3 minutes before the penne are ready to be drained. Sauté penne and zucchini in olive oil for a minute or so; add parsley and grated Parmesan cheese. Toss and serve immediately.

orecchiette with broccoli

ORECCHIETTE CON BROCCOLO

[6 SERVINGS]

1½ pounds broccoli (without stems)
 8 tablespoons olive oil
 ½ teaspoon hot red-pepper flakes
 1 pound orecchiette
   anchovy fillets (optional)
   salt and pepper

1. Parboil broccoli and sauté in oil with pepper flakes while orecchiette are cooking in boiling salted water.

2. When orecchiette are tender, drain and sauté together with broccoli in olive oil. Add anchovy fillets, if desired.

3. Salt and pepper to taste.

• This is a traditional pasta dish from the Puglia region, in southern Italy. Orecchiette (which means "little ears") are made from hard wheat flour and white flour, water, and salt and can be served with vegetables such as cauliflower, or with meat sauce.

risotto with spring vegetables

RISOTTO PRIMAVERA

[6 SERVINGS]

6 cups beef broth (see Basic
    Recipes, page 131)
2 tablespoons butter
1 small onion, chopped
2 cups Arborio rice
8 ounces white wine
    salt
    pepper, freshly ground
1 carrot, diced
1 celery stalk, chopped
½ red pepper and ½ yellow pepper,
    chopped
3½ ounces string beans, cut up
1 zucchini, diced
½ cup fresh green peas
5 tablespoons butter
4 tablespoons Parmesan cheese,
    grated
2 tablespoons parsley, minced
6 basil leaves, minced

1. Bring broth to a boil in a saucepan; reduce heat and simmer.

2. In another saucepan, melt 2 tablespoons butter; add onion and cook over moderate heat, stirring constantly with a wooden spoon until the onion has turned golden.

3. Add the rice and stir until every grain is coated with butter.

4. Add the wine and cook until it has almost evaporated. Season with salt and pepper.

5. Add the listed vegetables. Continue adding broth, 1 cup at a time, and continue stirring until all the liquid is absorbed. It will take about 20 minutes for the rice to absorb all the broth and to finish cooking.

6. Remove pan from heat and stir in the rest of the butter, Parmesan, parsley, and basil. Let stand for 2–3 minutes before serving.

7. Serve additional Parmesan cheese separately.

black squid ink risotto

RISOTTO NERO ALLE SEPPIE

[6 SERVINGS]

2½ pounds ink squid
   olive oil
1 onion, chopped
2 cloves garlic
1 cup white wine
2 tablespoons tomato sauce (see
   Basic Recipes, page 132)
6 cups fish stock (see Basic
   Recipes, page 131)
1 tablespoon butter
1 small onion, chopped
2 cups Arborio rice
1 cup white wine
   salt and pepper
1 tablespoon Parmesan cheese,
   grated
1 tablespoon olive oil
3 tablespoons parsley, minced

1. Squeeze out ink from its sacs and set aside the liquid.

2. Cut the squid into strips. Sauté them in olive oil with the onion and garlic. Discard all but the squid.

3. Add the ink and the white wine. Reduce. Add the tomato sauce. Remove from heat.

4. Meanwhile, prepare the risotto as in previous recipe, using fish stock in place of the beef broth. After 10 minutes, add the squid sauce, salt and pepper to taste, and continue cooking.

5. When cooked, remove pan from heat and stir in the Parmesan, olive oil, and parsley.

risotto with lemon and shrimp

RISOTTO AL LIMONE CON SCAMPI

[6 SERVINGS]

5 cups beef broth (see Basic
    Recipes, page 131)
8 tablespoons butter
2 cups Arborio rice
1 cup "canarino" (water in which 1
    lemon rind has been boiled)
1 lemon peel, grated
4 tablespoons Parmesan cheese,
    grated

SAUCE

  shrimp (6 or 7 per person)
  olive oil
1 cup white wine
3 tablespoons parsley, minced
1½ cups cream

GARNISH

  lemon strips
  parsley, minced

1. Bring broth to a boil in a saucepan; reduce heat and simmer.

2. In another saucepan, melt 2 tablespoons butter; add the rice and stir until every grain is coated with butter.

3. Begin to add broth slowly, one cup at a time, stirring until all liquid is absorbed and the rice is still moist.

4. After 10 minutes, substitute beef broth with lemon water and grated lemon peel. It will take about 20 minutes for the rice to absorb all the broth and to finish cooking.

5. Remove pan from heat and stir in the Parmesan cheese and the remaining 6 tablespoons of butter.

SAUCE

1. Sauté shrimp in oil.

2. Pour the white wine over and evaporate.

3. Add the parsley and cream. Reduce.

4. On each plate, place shrimp over risotto and garnish with lemon strips and parsley, as in photo.

fish

PESCI

At the break of

dawn as the first sun rays appear, the lake turns from dark blue-green to light gray-blue with silver overtones, and the scales of the fish in the basket, placed at the boat landing, shimmer in the morning light.

fish

Fresh Salmon Carpaccio with Porcini Mushroom Salad
CARPACCIO DI SALMONE CON INSALATINA DI FUNGHI PORCINI

Grilled Salmon with Peppers
SALMONE ALLA GRIGLIA CON PEPERONI

Marinated Sturgeon
STORIONE MARINATO

Sturgeon Wrapped in Lettuce and Served with a Saffron Sauce
STORIONE AVVOLTO CON LATTUGA IN SALSA ZAFFERANO

Turbot Fillet with Zucchini and Potatoes
BIANCO DI ROMBO CON ZUCCHINE E PATATE

Perch Fillets with Fried Vegetables
FILETTI DI PESCE PERSICO CON VERDURA CROCCANTE

Shrimp with Artichokes and Fried Zucchini
SCAMPI SU FONDI DI CARCIOFI CON ZUCCHINE FRITTE

Sea Bass in Sparkling Wine
BRANZINO ALLO SPUMANTE

Monkfish with Turnip
CODA DI ROSPO CON RAPE

Warm Seafood Pastry Puffs
SFOGLIATINE TIEPIDE AI FRUTTI DI MARE

fresh salmon carpaccio with porcini mushroom salad

CARPACCIO DI SALMONE CON INSALATINA DI FUNGHI PORCINI

[1 SERVING]

6 basil leaves
olive oil
lemon juice
3 ounces fresh salmon, cleaned
and thinly sliced
1½ ounces fresh porcini mushrooms,
thinly sliced (if unavailable,
use champignons)
salt and pepper, freshly ground
salad greens
1 ounce Parmesan cheese,
shredded

GARNISH

4 basil leaves
parsley
tomato, diced

1. Blend the 6 basil leaves with the olive oil and lemon juice. Use this to marinate the salmon for a couple of minutes.

2. Season the mushrooms with olive oil, lemon juice, salt, and pepper.

3. Spread the salad greens on the plate, cover with salmon, top with the sliced mushrooms and in the center, arrange the Parmesan.

4. Garnish with basil, parsley, and diced tomato.

grilled **salmon** with **peppers**

SALMONE ALLA GRIGLIA CON PEPERONI

[6 SERVINGS]

2 pounds fresh salmon steaks
  olive oil
  herbs for marinade: sage,
    rosemary, thyme, marjoram,
    and bay leaf
  salt and pepper, freshly ground
2 red peppers
2 yellow peppers
2 green peppers
  garlic
  anchovy fillets

SAUCE

1 small onion, chopped
  olive oil
6 plum tomatoes parboiled,
    peeled, seeded, and diced
1 red pepper, seeded and diced
  basil leaves
  salt
  pepper, freshly ground

1. Marinate the salmon steaks in the olive oil and herbs for about 1 hour.

2. Grill with a little salt and pepper.

3. In the meantime, roast the peppers in the oven until they become completely black. Peel, remove caps and seeds, and shape into leaves. Finish cooking the peppers in olive oil with garlic and anchovy fillets.

SAUCE

1. Sauté onion in oil and add tomatoes, the red pepper, basil, salt, and pepper. When cooked, blend in a blender.

2. Arrange salmon, peppers, and sauce as in photo.

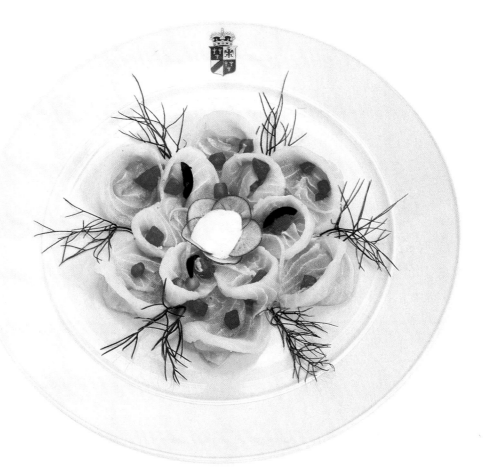

marinated **sturgeon**

STORIONE MARINATO

[6 SERVINGS]

1¾ pounds sturgeon, thinly sliced
olive oil
juice of 2 lemons, freshly
   squeezed
salt
pepper, freshly ground
dill sprigs

GARNISH
radish
mayonnaise (see Basic Recipes,
   page 134)
olives
strips of lemon rind
6 marinated tomatoes (see Basic
   Recipes, page 133)
dill

1. Marinate the sturgeon fillets for 15 minutes in olive oil, lemon juice, salt, pepper, and dill.

2. Remove sturgeon fillets and roll up each one individually. Place under broiler for 1 minute or so.

3. Sprinkle with oil and lemon; arrange on plates.

4. Arrange with sliced radish and mayonnaise in the center. Add chopped olives, lemon rind, the marinated tomatoes, and dill, as in photo.

sturgeon **wrapped** in **lettuce** and **served** with a **saffron** sauce

STORIONE AVVOLTO CON LATTUGA IN SALSA ZAFFERANO

[6 SERVINGS]

6 ounces lettuce, parboiled
1½ pounds sturgeon, clean and cut
    into slices
    salt and pepper

FISH CREAM SAUCE

3 cups fish stock (see Basic
    Recipes, page 131)
3 tablespoons cream
2 teaspoons butter
1 teaspoon saffron (powdered)

MUSHROOM PUREE

1½ pounds porcini mushrooms,
    sliced
6 tablespoons olive oil
6 garlic cloves
3 cups white wine
1 cup brown sauce (see Basic
    Recipes, page 133)

GARNISH

3 plum tomatoes, parboiled,
    peeled, and diced
6 parsley springs
6 teaspoons saffron threads

1. On 6 separate sheets of plastic wrap, spread the lettuce leaves; place the sturgeon over lettuce. Add salt and pepper, roll up the plastic wrap and tie up the ends.

2. Steam fish rolls for about 10 minutes. Remove plastic wrap. Cut each roll into 6 slices.

3. In the meantime, prepare the fish cream sauce: heat the fish stock; add cream. Reduce; add butter and saffron. Stir until sauce is smooth and creamy.

4. To prepare the mushroom puree, sauté the porcini mushrooms in olive oil with the garlic cloves (these can be removed later); add the wine and the brown sauce. Reduce; blend in a blender.

5. On each plate, place 6 slices of sturgeon over the fish cream sauce. Garnish with the mushroom puree, using a pastry bag. Add the diced tomatoes and parsley; sprinkle with the saffron threads.

turbot **fillet** with **zucchini** and **potatoes**

BIANCO DI ROMBO CON ZUCCHINE E PATATE

[1 SERVING]

7	ounces potatoes, thinly sliced
2	medium zucchini, thinly sliced
4–5	ounces fillet of turbot
	salt and pepper
	basil leaves
1	tomato, parboiled, peeled, and diced after removing inner pulp and seeds
	olive oil
2	tablespoons fish stock (see Basic Recipes, page 131)
	butter

1. Overlap slices of potato into a buttered oven dish.

2. Layer the zucchini on top.

3. Place the slightly salted and peppered fillet on the zucchini, and top with the basil and diced tomato.

4. Sprinkle with olive oil and fish stock.

5. Place in a preheated oven for 10 minutes at 450°.

6. When cooked, remove turbot and set aside. Arrange vegetables on a plate; place the turbot on top and pour sauce over.

7. To prepare the sauce, blend the leftover juices with butter.

perch **fillets** with **fried** vegetables

FILETTI DI PESCE PERSICO CON VERDURA CROCCANTE

[6 SERVINGS]

1½ pounds perch fillets
  flour
2 eggs, beaten
  salt
  butter
  fresh sage
1 pound vegetables: zucchini and
    eggplant (cut lengthwise with
    pulp and seeds removed, keep-
    ing only the skin), red pepper
    (cut lengthwise with cap and
    seeds removed), carrot, onion,
    and leek, all cut into thin strips

BATTER
flour and cornstarch in
  equal quantities
beer
olive oil

GARNISH
6 tomatoes, shaped into roses
  parsley, minced

1. Dip fillets in flour, then in beaten eggs seasoned with salt. Sauté in butter with sage.

2. Dip the vegetables in the batter of flour and cornstarch diluted with beer, and fry the vegetables in olive oil.

3. Arrange 4 or 5 perch fillets on each plate together with fried vegetables.

4. Place rose in the center and use minced parsley around the border.

shrimp with artichokes and fried zucchini

SCAMPI SU FONDO DI CARCIOFI CON ZUCCHINE FRITTE

[6 SERVINGS]

6 artichokes
  bread crumbs
  Parmesan cheese, grated
  rosemary, chopped
  basil leaves, chopped
6–9 shrimp (depending on size)
  butter
1 tablespoon shallots, finely
  chopped
½ cup brandy
1 cup white wine
6 large zucchini
  milk
  flour
  olive oil

GARNISH
lemon slices
parsley

1. Discard all artichoke leaves and boil only the bottom parts in water and lemon.

2. Combine bread crumbs, Parmesan, and herbs and spread over the artichoke bottoms.

3. Sauté shrimp in butter. Remove fat; add shallots. Cook briefly over high heat with brandy and white wine. Reduce.

4. After removing pulp and seeds of zucchini, cut the outer part in pencil-thin strips, soak in milk, dip in flour, and fry in olive oil.

5. Place shrimp in the center of each plate. Arrange the zucchini.

6. Garnish with lemon slices and parsley.

sea bass in sparkling wine

BRANZINO ALLO SPUMANTE

[6 SERVINGS]

2 pounds sea bass, sliced into 6
    steaks
½ pound mushrooms
    (champignons), sliced
6 tablespoons marinated tomatoes
    (see Basic Recipes, page 133)
    salt
    pepper, freshly ground
1 bottle Spumante (sparkling wine)
8 tablespoons cream
1 egg yolk
2 tablespoons of whipped cream
    vegetable assortment: steamed
    potatoes, carrots, and zucchini

1. Place sea bass steaks in a pan; cover with mushrooms, marinated toma-toes, salt, and pepper. Pour the sparkling wine over.

2. Cover pan with aluminum foil; place in oven at 400° for 8 minutes. When cooked, remove fish and reduce juice.

3. Add the cream and reduce until sauce is smooth and creamy.

4. Remove from stove and whisk the whipped cream with the egg yolk; add to the sauce.

5. Pour this over the fish and return to the oven under the broiler.

6. Arrange as in photo, with steamed vegetables on the side.

monkfish with turnip

CODA DI ROSPO CON RAPE

[6 SERVINGS]

6 small turnips
1 cup light cream
  salt
  nutmeg, freshly grated
1½ pounds monkfish, cleaned
  flour
  paprika
  olive oil
  butter
3 small zucchini, sliced
  olive oil
  thyme

GARNISH
marinated tomatoes (see Basic
  Recipes, page 133)
tomato, sliced
chives

1. Slice turnips very thinly; sauté with cream, salt, and nutmeg for 3-4 minutes.

2. Overlap turnip slices on individual plates and cover with leftover cream. Broil.

3. Cut fish into medallions, dip in flour mixed with a pinch of paprika, and sauté in oil and butter.

4. Place the fish over the bed of turnips.

5. In the meantime, sauté the zucchini in oil and sprinkle with thyme.

6. Arrange zucchini in the center with the slices of tomato. Decorate with marinated tomatoes and chives.

warm seafood pastry puffs

SFOGLIATINE TIEPIDE AI FRUTTI DI MARE

[6 SERVINGS]

 2 pounds puff pastry
 1 egg
1½ pounds mussels with shells
1½ pounds clams with shells
1½ cups olive oil
 1 garlic clove
½ cup white wine
10 ounces fillet of sole
½ pound medium shrimp, cleaned
½ pound jumbo shrimp, cleaned
 5 ounces spider-crab meat
   (granseola)
   choice of salad greens
   juice of 1½ lemons, freshly
    squeezed
   salt
   pepper, freshly ground

GARNISH
6 parsley sprigs
6 radishes shaped into flowers

1. Roll out the puff pastry as thinly as possible to obtain, for each serving, 6 circles with a diameter of 6 inches. With a cutter, form 6 rose petals out of each circle, discarding the edges and leaving the center intact. Brush with a beaten egg and place in a preheated oven at 425° for about 15 minutes.

2. Clean mussels and clams and sauté in a pan with ½ cup of oil and garlic. Pour in the wine. When the shells open, the fish is cooked.

3. Remove mussels and clams from shells, discarding those that did not open.

4. Parboil separately fillets of sole and shrimp for about 1 minute. Hollow out the center of each "petal" with a teaspoon; place over the salad greens already arranged on the plate.

5. Fill each "petal" with the 6 varieties of fish seasoned with the remaining cup of oil, lemon juice, salt, and pepper. Decorate the center with parsley sprigs and radishes.

RIGHT: THE NAPOLEON ROOM

meats

CARNI

The Grill, with its informal ambiance, offers regional cuisine in an intimate setting.

Beef Carpaccio with Aromatic Herbs and Rucola
CARPACCIO ALLE ERBE AROMATICHE CON RUCOLA

Veal Carpaccio with Braised Trevisana Salad
CARPACCIO DI VITELLO CON TREVISANA BRASATA

Three Fillets Villa d'Este Style
TRE FILETTI VILLA D'ESTE

Beef Fillet with Glazed Onions
FILETTO DI MANZO CON CIPOLLINE GLASSATE

Beef Fillet in Bread Crust
FILETTO DI MANZO IN CROSTA DI PANE

Beef Tenderloin with Asparagus Tips and Artichoke
FILETTO DI BUE CON PUNTE DI ASPARAGI E CARCIOFI

Florentine T-Bone Steak with Beans
COSTATA ALLA FIORENTINA CON FAGIOLI

Stuffed Lamb Cutlets with Pears and Potato Dumplings
COSTINE DI AGNELLO FARCITE CON PERE AL MIRTILLO E GNOCCO DI PATATE

Rack of Lamb with Mint
CARRÈ DI AGNELLO ALLA MENTA

Milanese Veal Cutlet with Vegetable Casserole
COSTOLETTA ALLA MILANESE CON PEPERONATA

Veal Scaloppine with Calf's Kidney and Risotto al Salto
SCALOPPINE CON ROGNONE E RISOTTO AL SALTO

Stuffed Veal Medallions and Eggplant Parmigiana
MEDAGLIONI DI VITELLO FARCITI E MELANZANA PARMIGIANA

Veal Piccata in White Wine Sauce with Broad Beans
PICCATA AL VINO BIANCO CON FAVE

Veal Piccata with Lemon and Vegetable Flan
FILETTO DI VITELLO AL LIMONE CON SFORMATO DI VERDURE

Ossobuco Gremolada with Risotto Milanese Style
OSSOBUCO GREMOLADA CON RISOTTO ALLA MILANESE

Chicken Breast "Arlecchino"
PETTO DI POLLO ARLECCHINO

Roasted Baby Chicken Marinated with Lemon, Garlic, and Thyme
GALLETTO CROCCANTE CON LIMONE, AGLIO E TIMO

Breast of Duck with Lemon, Honey, and Pine Nuts
PETTO DI ANATRA IN AGRO-DOLCE CON PINOLI

Calf's Brains with Marinated Tomatoes
CERVELLA DORATA CON POMODORI MARINATI

Calf's Liver Venetian Style with Polenta
FEGATO ALLA VENEZIANA CON POLENTA

beef **carpaccio** with aromatic **herbs** and **rucola**

CARPACCIO ALLE ERBE AROMATICHE CON RUCOLA

[6 SERVINGS]

2 teaspoons mustard
2 tablespoons wine vinegar
3 tablespoons extra-virgin olive oil
   salt
   pepper, freshly ground
18 very thin slices of beef fillet
3 ounces Parmesan cheese, sliced
2 ounces rucola sprouts
½ pound rucola salad
8 ounces porcini mushrooms,
   very thinly sliced (if unavailable,
   use champignons)

MARINADE

6 tablespoons extra-virgin olive oil
   juice of 1 lemon, freshly squeezed
⅓ cup chopped fresh herbs:
   chives, tarragon, marjoram,
   and thyme

1. In a small bowl, dilute mustard with vinegar and whisk while slowly adding olive oil.

2. Add salt and pepper to taste. Pour over the mushrooms, rucola, and rucola sprouts.

3. Place the beef slices flat on a large platter and marinate for 2 minutes with the lemon juice, 6 tablespoons of olive oil, and the herbs.

4. Over a few slices of Parmesan, arrange each slice of beef to resemble a rose. Use 3 slices of beef for each plate.

5. Form 3 small mounds of mushrooms; place together with the rucola sprouts between the beef and over the rucola salad.

6. In the center of the plate, arrange the mushroom slices in the shape of a flower; upon it, place a tomato peel shaped like a small rose.

veal **carpaccio** with **braised** trevisana **salad**

CARPACCIO DI VITELLO CON TREVISANA BRASATA

[6 SERVINGS]

1 tablespoon shallots, chopped
1 cup extra-virgin olive oil
3 heads of Trevisana (radicchio di Treviso)
3 juniper berries
1 heaping tablespoon sugar
  salt
2 teaspoons green peppercorns
½ cup red wine vinegar
2 cups red wine
½ cup dry vermouth
  juice of 2 lemons, freshly squeezed
1 pound veal, very thinly sliced (5 or 6 slices per person)

GARNISH
celery stalks
white truffle from Alba

1. Sauté shallots in 1 tablespoon oil. Add Trevisana, sliced lengthwise. Add juniper berries, sugar, salt, and peppercorns.

2. Pour in vinegar, wine, and vermouth, one at a time; wait until almost evaporated before pouring in next liquid. Cook for at least 10 minutes. Remove Trevisana and reduce sauce.

3. Pass sauce through a sieve; add remaining oil with lemon juice.

4. Beat with a whisk, and add salt to taste.

5. Arrange the food on the plate as shown, topping off the meat with a small shaving of truffle. Serve the sauce at the table.

• Carpaccio meat is normally served raw; however, if desired, it can also be served warm by placing the plate under the broiler for a couple of minutes before adding the truffle.
• The gravy boat in the photo contains the sauce in which the Trevisana salad was braised.

88

the **three** fillets **villa d'este** style

TRE FILETTI VILLA D'ESTE

[6 SERVINGS]

6 medium potatoes, thinly sliced
  butter
6 2-ounce veal fillets
6 2-ounce beef fillets
6 2-ounce lamb fillets
  butter and olive oil

BEARNAISE SAUCE (for beef)
2 tablespoons white wine
2 tablespoons tarragon vinegar
2 tablespoons dried tarragon
1 tablespoon shallots, finely chopped
  salt
  pepper, freshly ground
3 tablespoons water
3 egg yolks
½ pound butter

CAPER SAUCE (for veal)
  garlic, minced
  olive oil
24 capers
6 olives, chopped
6 tablespoons tomato sauce (see
  Basic Recipes, page 132)

MUSHROOM SAUCE (for lamb)
1 garlic clove
1 tablespoons olive oil
3 ounces porcini mushrooms, sliced
½ teaspoon salt
  parsley, chopped

First prepare the sauces.

BEARNAISE SAUCE

In a non-aluminum saucepan, bring to a boil wine, vinegar, tarragon, shallots, salt, and pepper. Stir with a wooden spoon until all liquid evaporates. Lower flame; add water and egg yolks. Stir briskly with a whisk until the sauce has thickened to the consistency of mayonnaise. In another saucepan, melt butter and add it slowly, in a thin stream, to the egg mixture. Set aside.

CAPER SAUCE

Sauté garlic in olive oil; add capers, olives, and tomato sauce. Cook until heated through.

MUSHROOM SAUCE

Sauté garlic in olive oil until golden. Add mushrooms and salt; cook until all liquid is absorbed. At the last moment, add parsley.

1. Slice potatoes very thinly. Cover with butter; place under broiler for 2 minutes.

2. Discard butter and transfer potatoes onto each plate, forming 3 circles, as in photo.

3. Sauté fillets in butter and oil, according to taste. Place each fillet on the rounds of overlapped potatoes; top with the sauces and pass under broiler.

89

beef **fillet** with **glazed** onions

FILETTO DI MANZO CON CIPOLLINE GLASSATE

[6 SERVINGS]

2 pounds beef fillets
  salt
1 tablespoon black peppercorns,
  crushed
  olive oil
1 tablespoon shallots, finely
  chopped
1 cup red wine
2 tablespoons brown sauce (see
  Basic Recipes, page 133)

1 pound potatoes
2 tablespoons onion, chopped
  olive oil
  butter
3 slices prosciutto crudo, cut
  into strips
2 tablespoons butter
1 tablespoon sugar
1 bay leaf
1 pound pearl onions, peeled and
  washed
  pinch of salt
½ cup dry white wine
½ cup beef broth
1 bunch grapes

1. Cut fillets into 6 portions. Sprinkle each fillet with salt and peppercorns; sauté them in oil. Remove meat and fat.

2. In a large dish, place a smaller dish upside-down. Place all fillets on top of and in the center of the upside-down dish; wait for liquid to drip and collect on the border of the larger dish.

3. Add shallots to pan in which meat was cooked. Pour in wine; reduce. Add to pan the liquid from the larger dish; reduce. Add brown sauce. Finish cooking.

4. Boil the potatoes until tender. When cool, peel and slice into matchsticks.

5. Sauté onion in olive oil and butter. Add potatoes and julienne of prosciutto crudo. Turn over like an omelette; sauté until a golden crust is formed on both sides.

6. To glaze the pearl onions, melt butter with sugar and bay leaf in a saucepan (preferably, earthenware); add onions. Cook on high heat for about 3 minutes. Sprinkle with salt. Pour in wine; when half-evaporated, add broth. Lower heat, stir gently, and cover. Cook until onions are light brown.

7. Peel grapes and stir in pan with a little butter.

8. When serving, fillets can be sliced (the photo shows a serving of fillet for 2 persons) and spread over the sauce with the grapes, potatoes, and onions on the side.

beef **fillet** in **bread** crust

FILETTO DI MANZO IN CROSTA DI PANE

[6 SERVINGS]

olive oil
2 pounds beef fillets
salt and pepper
about 10 slices of prosciutto crudo

BREAD CRUST

14 ounces flour
2 eggs
2 tablespoons white wine vinegar
salt
water for kneading

STUFFING

3½ ounces mushrooms
(champignons, thinly sliced and
cooked with chopped basil)
2 ounces spinach, cooked,
strained, and finely chopped
2 ounces cooked ham, pureed
2 egg yolks
egg, beaten
potatoes, sliced lengthwise
zucchini, eggplant, and red
peppers, diced
olive oil
salt and pepper, freshly ground

1. Salt and pepper the beef fillet. In olive oil, sauté until browned.

2. Next, make the dough for the bread crust: mix flour with the eggs, the vinegar, a little salt, and enough water to knead. Make a ball of the dough, cover with a damp cloth, and allow it to rest for about half an hour. Then roll out until at least 2½ inches wider than the fillet.

3. Over a sheet of foil, spread slices of prosciutto crudo.

4. Prepare the stuffing: combine mushrooms, spinach, and cooked ham. Add egg yolks and mix. Spread this over the prosciutto crudo. Place the beef over the stuffing. Roll up and transfer to the dough. Roll up the dough, press it at the seams, and seal it with the beaten egg.

5. Place in a preheated oven at 400° for about 40 minutes.

6. Potatoes can be roasted or sautéed, and zucchini, eggplant, and peppers should be sautéed in oil with salt and pepper.

beef **tenderloin** with **asparagus tips** and **artichokes**

FILETTO DI BUE CON PUNTE DI ASPARAGI E CARCIOFI

[6 SERVINGS]

48 asparagus stalks
12 artichokes
   juice of 1½ lemons
½ cup olive oil
   garlic (optional)
¾ cup beef broth (see Basic
      Recipe, page 131)
3 teaspoons parsley, chopped
6 beef fillets (7 ounces each)
2 tablespoons butter
½ cup Madeira wine
¼ cup brown sauce (see Basic
      Recipes, page 133)
18 slices Parmesan cheese
3 plum tomatoes, diced
30 long slivers of parboiled carrots
6 tomatoes shaped into roses

1. Boil asparagus for 10 minutes.

2. Clean artichokes and cut into quarters; sprinkle with lemon juice to prevent darkening. Sauté artichokes in a tablespoon of olive oil with garlic, if using; add beef broth and parsley. Cook for about 15 minutes.

3. Blend half the cooked artichokes. Reserve the other half for decoration.

4. Sauté the fillets in remaining olive oil and butter, according to taste. Remove fillets and fat, and pour the Madeira wine into the pan; add brown sauce and simmer until reduced. At the last moment, add a teaspoon of butter to bind the sauce.

5. When ready to serve, decorate the fillets, placed over the Madeira sauce, with the artichoke mixture. Add 3 slices of Parmesan, 3 asparagus tips, and diced tomatoes.

6. The remaining asparagus and artichokes, along with the carrots and tomato roses, can be arranged as in photo.

florentine t-bone steak with beans

COSTATA ALLA FIORENTINA CON FAGIOLI

[1 SERVING]

10½ ounce T-bone steak
  sage
  rosemary
  thyme
  lemon slices
  onion slices
  bay leaf
  olive oil
  salt and pepper, freshly ground

STUFFED TOMATO

1 tomato
  onion, chopped
  olive oil
  parsley, chopped
  bread crumbs
  salt

BEANS

½ pound cannellini beans
  cloves
  celery stalk
  sage
  olive oil
  black pepper, freshly ground
  onion, sliced

  Trevisana (radicchio di Treviso)
    salad
  olive oil
  salt and pepper, freshly ground

STEAK

1. Marinate the T-bone steak for 1 hour in oil, sage, rosemary, thyme, lemon slices, onion slices, and bay leaf.

2. Sprinkle steak with salt and pepper and grill.

TOMATO

1. Cut off the top of the tomato. Remove pulp and set aside. Turn tomato upside-down to remove liquid.

2. Sauté onion in olive oil; combine with parsley and bread crumbs. Add the reserved pulp. Salt the inside of the tomato, fill it with the pulp mixture, and place in oven (450°) for about 5 minutes.

BEANS

1. Boil beans in water with cloves, celery, and sage.

2. When tender, season with oil and several twists of pepper and raw onion slices.

3. Grill the Trevisana salad with oil, salt, and pepper. Arrange on plate with the steak, beans, and tomato.

93

stuffed lamb cutlets with pears and potato dumplings

COSTINE DI AGNELLO FARCITE CON PERE AL MIRTILLO E GNOCCO DI PATATE

[6 SERVINGS]

6 lamb cutlets
STUFFING
½ pound veal, ground
2 ounces spinach, cooked, strained, and finely chopped
2 ounces mushrooms, sliced and sautéed
1 egg
1 tablespoon foie gras
   shaving of white truffle
2 eggs
   bread crumbs
   butter
   olive oil
PEARS
3 pears
   white wine, enough to cover pears
   cinnamon
   cloves
   cranberries
DUMPLINGS
7 ounces potatoes
2 ounces flour
1 tablespoon Parmesan cheese, grated
1 egg
   butter
½ teaspoon sugar
   cinnamon
6 stewed prunes

1. Slice the cutlets in half lengthwise and spread the 2 sides apart, pounding gently to flatten.

2. Combine veal, spinach, mushrooms, egg, cream, foie gras, and truffle.

3. Spread the mixture inside each cutlet and reshape. Dip in seasoned beaten eggs and cover with bread crumbs.

4. In a large frying pan, heat butter and oil. When oil is hot, sauté cutlets for about 5 minutes on each side, until golden brown and crisp.

5. Cook pears in white wine with cinnamon and cloves. Remove pears and halve them. Reduce the liquid in which the pears cooked and add the cranberries. Fill each pear with the cranberries.

DUMPLINGS

1. Boil potatoes. Peel and mash. Add flour, Parmesan, and egg. Mix without kneading. Spread out and make 12 discs, ½ inch in diameter; sandwich each prune between 2 discs.

2. Cook dumplings in boiling salted water. Drain. Sauté in butter with sugar and cinnamon.

94

rack of lamb with mint

CARRÈ DI AGNELLO ALLA MENTA

[6 SERVINGS]

olive oil
onion, carrot, and celery stalk,
    finely chopped
mint leaves
1 cup Hollandaise sauce
4½ pounds rack of lamb
    salt and pepper, freshly ground
3 tablespoons white wine vinegar
⅓ cup white wine

HOLLANDAISE SAUCE

½ pound butter
4 egg yolks
2 tablespoons lemon juice
¼ teaspoon salt
    pinch cayenne
2 tablespoons butter
1 tablespoon sugar
1 bay leaf
1 pound pearl onions, peeled and
    washed
    pinch of salt
½ cup dry white wine
½ cup beef broth
    carrots, boiled
    string beans, boiled

1. Sauté onion, carrot, celery, and a few mint leaves in oil for 5–8 minutes; add salted and peppered lamb and sprinkle with vinegar; when vinegar has evaporated, add wine. Place in a preheated oven at 450° for 10 minutes.

2. Remove the lamb and pass the vegetables through a sieve. Discard the vegetables, reserving the liquid for the sauce.

HOLLANDAISE

1. Heat the butter to bubbling, but do not let brown. Pour egg yolks, lemon juice, salt, and cayenne into blender container. Blend on low speed and quickly pour in the hot butter in a steady stream. Keep the Hollandaise warm in a double boiler.

2. To glaze the pearl onions, melt butter with sugar and bay leaf in a saucepan (preferably, earthenware) and add onions.

3. Cook on high heat for about 3 minutes. Sprinkle with salt. Pour in the wine; when half evaporated, add broth.

4. Lower flame, stir gently, and cover. Cook until onions are light brown.

5. Slice the rack of lamb into cutlets (2 or 3 per person), cover with Hollandaise, and broil in the oven.

6. Spread vegetable sauce on each plate; add cutlets.

7. Serve with boiled carrots and string beans sautéed in butter and glazed pearl onions.

milanese veal cutlet
with **vegetable** casserole

COSTOLETTA ALLA MILANESE CON PEPERONATA

[6 SERVINGS]

6 veal cutlets
1 cup milk
2 eggs, beaten
  salt and pepper, freshly ground
  bread crumbs
  butter and olive oil
1 red pepper
1 yellow pepper
2 medium eggplants
3 or 4 zucchini
2 red onions
1 pound tomatoes
1 cup olive oil
  salt and pepper, freshly ground

GARNISH
a cornucopia made out of an
  omelette

1. Pound veal until quite flat. Place slices in a shallow platter and cover with milk; allow to stand for about 10 minutes. Drain and dry well. Dip in eggs seasoned with salt and pepper and cover each slice with bread crumbs.

2. In a large frying pan, heat butter and oil. When hot, sauté cutlets for about 5 minutes on each side until golden brown and crisp. Transfer to a plate.

VEGETABLE CASSEROLE

1. Seed and cut peppers into strips. Coarsely chop or dice unpeeled eggplants and zucchini. Slice onions. Quarter unpeeled tomatoes and save the juices.

2. Heat olive oil and add vegetables; if available, use an earthenware pot. Season with salt and pepper and cook for about 10 minutes, until softened. At the end of the cooking time, add tomatoes with their juices. Stir, cover, and cook for about 30 minutes on low heat.

3. Serve vegetables alongside veal cutlet, with omelette cornucopia, if desired.

veal **scaloppine** with **calf's** kidney and **risotto** al **salto**

SCALOPPINE CON ROGNONE E RISOTTO AL SALTO

[6 SERVINGS]

18 calf's kidney slices (1 ounce
   each)
   juice of 2 lemons
18 veal scaloppine (1 ounce each)
   olive oil and butter
 1 cup white wine
 1 cup cream
3½ ounces gorgonzola cheese
   salt and pepper, freshly ground

RISOTTO AL SALTO
 3 cups Milanese Risotto (see
   recipe, page 101)

GARNISH
saffron threads
chives

1. Soak kidneys in warm water for about 30 minutes with juice of 1 lemon. Drain, pat dry, and cut into thin slices, removing all the inside suet.

2. Sauté veal and kidney in oil and butter until cooked, for only a few minutes.

3. Remove veal and kidney and scrape away the fat.

4. Add wine to pan; reduce. Add the cream and the juice of the second lemon. At the last moment, stir in gorgonzola cheese.

RISOTTO AL SALTO

1. Heat a nonstick pan, melt a tablespoon of butter and flatten out the risotto with a wooden spoon until it is thin as a pancake. Let it sauté over medium heat until a golden brown crust is formed underneath; check by slightly lifting an edge. Turn it over with the edge of a lid or dish.

2. Slip the fried rice back into the pan so that it becomes quite crisp on both sides.

3. Make one portion at a time. Turn the "risotto al salto" over onto its plate.

4. Place the risotto al salto on each plate beneath the veal and kidney; top with the gorgonzola sauce. Decorate with saffron threads and chopped chives.

stuffed veal medallions and eggplant parmigiana

MEDAGLIONI DI VITELLO FARCITI E MELANZANE PARMIGIANA

[6 SERVINGS]

36 small veal slices (about 1 ounce each)

STUFFING

1 pound assorted vegetables, sliced and chopped
18 slices prosciutto crudo
2 or 3 eggs
   salt and pepper, freshly ground
   bread crumbs
   olive oil and butter
18 slices mozzarella cheese

EGGPLANT PARMIGIANA

3 eggplants
   salt
   flour
   olive oil
8 ounces mozzarella cheese, diced
3 tablespoons Parmesan cheese, grated
1 cup tomato sauce (see Basic Recipes, page 132)
   basil and oregano

1. Sauté vegetables until "al dente" and place a spoonful of vegetables on each slice of prosciutto. Wrap up and sandwich between 2 slices of veal. With a meat pounder, shape into rounds. Dip in seasoned beaten eggs and cover with bread crumbs.

2. In a large frying pan, heat butter and oil.

3. When hot, sauté medallions for about 5 minutes on each side until golden brown and crisp.

4. Top with mozzarella and place under a broiler for a few minutes.

EGGPLANT PARMIGIANA

1. Slice eggplants lengthwise. Salt and place under a heavy weight to eliminate all liquid.

2. Wipe and dry eggplant slices.

3. Sprinkle eggplants with flour and fry in olive oil. Fill each slice with mozzarella, Parmesan, tomato sauce, and the herbs.

4. Roll up each slice and heat in oven.

veal **piccata** in **white wine** with **broad** beans

PICCATA AL VINO BIANCO CON FAVE

[6 SERVINGS]

18 veal slices (3 per person), about
     1½ ounces each
     salt and pepper, freshly ground
     olive oil and butter
     fresh sage
3 slices prosciutto crudo
1 cup dry white wine
6 red peppers
3 small Italian sausages or
     ground pork
     bread crumbs
1 egg
2 tablespoons parsley, chopped
     salt and pepper, freshly ground
     beef broth (see Basic Recipes,
        page 131)
½ pound broad beans

1. Sprinkle the veal slices with salt and pepper and sauté them in olive oil, butter, and sage.

2. Remove meat and scrape the fat from the pan. Add the prosciutto crudo, cut into strips.

3. Add wine; reduce. Stir in 1 tablespoon of butter to bind. Remove caps and seeds from peppers. Combine sausage, bread crumbs, egg, and parsley. Season with salt and pepper.

4. Fill the peppers with the sausage mixture and cover with broth.

5. Place in the oven at 350° for 30 minutes.

6. Boil broad beans and sauté in butter.

veal **piccata** with **lemon** and **vegetable** flan

FILETTO DI VITELLO AL LIMONE CON SFORMATO DI VERDURE

[6 SERVINGS]

2 (2-ounce) veal fillets per person
  salt and pepper, freshly ground
  olive oil and butter
1 cup white wine
  juice of 1 lemon
  brown sauce (see Basic
    Recipes, page 133)
3 lemons
1 tablespoon butter
1 tablespoon sugar

VEGETABLE FLAN

2 ounces each of string beans,
    carrots, cauliflower, zucchini,
    and celery, coarsely chopped
    and boiled
1 cup milk
4 eggs
¼ cup flour
  salt and pepper, freshly ground
  nutmeg, freshly ground

¾ pound string beans
  butter
  almonds, toasted

GARNISH

3 tablespoons marinated
    tomatoes (see Basic Recipes,
    page 133)

1. Sauté veal, slightly salted and peppered, in olive oil and butter. Add wine and lemon juice; reduce. Remove veal and scrape fat from pan.

2. Place veal fillets on an inverted dish on top of a larger dish to collect the liquid that will drip onto the border of the larger dish. Collect liquid and return it to the pan.

3. Add brown sauce; reduce by half. Add butter to bind.

4. Cut the rinds of 2 lemons into strips. Boil these in water.

5. In another pan, combine lemon rinds with butter and sugar until lemon rinds begin to caramelize. Peel and slice the remaining lemon and also slice the 2 lemons without the rind to use for decoration.

6. For the vegetable flan, puree all the ingredients in a food processor. Grease and flour 6 small molds. Pour in the mixture. Place the molds in a pan containing water and bake in a preheated oven at 375° for 30–35 minutes.

7. Boil string beans and sauté them in butter. Garnish with almonds.

8. Spread the veal sauce on half the plate and place the fillets on top. Place the caramelized lemon rinds and the lemon slices on top of the fillets. Sprinkle the marinated tomatoes on the vegetable flan.

ossobuco **gremolada** with **risotto** milanese **style**

OSSOBUCO GREMOLADA CON RISOTTO ALLA MILANESE

[6 SERVINGS]

- 6 ossibuchi (veal shanks) with bone and marrow
  salt and pepper, freshly ground
  flour
- 2 tablespoons butter
- 2 tablespoons olive oil
  carrot, onion, celery, finely chopped (1 tablespoon each)
- 1 cup dry white wine
- 2–3 tablespoons tomato sauce (see Basic Recipes, page 132)
- 1 cup beef broth (see Basic Recipes, page 131)
- 3 tablespoons parsley, chopped
- 1 large garlic clove, crushed
- 1 lemon rind, grated

MILANESE RISOTTO

- 6 cups beef broth (see Basic Recipes, page 131)
- 7 tablespoons butter
- 1 small onion, finely chopped
- 2 cups Arborio rice
- ½ cup white wine
- ½ teaspoon saffron
- 3 tablespoons Parmesan cheese, grated
  salt and pepper, freshly ground

1. Salt and pepper the veal and coat with flour. Heat the butter and oil and brown the meat.

2. Remove the meat and add carrot, onion, and celery. Sauté. Add wine; reduce. Return the meat to the saucepan. Add tomato sauce and broth; cover and cook gently until tender. Cooking time varies according to the quality of the meat but should take about 1½ hours.

3. Just before serving, mix parsley, garlic, and lemon rind together and add to the sauce. Simmer.

4. To make the risotto, bring broth to a boil in a saucepan, then reduce heat and simmer.

5. In another saucepan, melt 6 tablespoons of butter; add chopped onion, and cook over moderate heat, stirring constantly with a wooden spoon until onion has turned golden.

6. Add rice and stir for about 3 minutes so that every grain is coated with the butter. Add the wine and let it evaporate. Add 1 cup of boiling broth and continue stirring until the liquid is absorbed. Keep adding broth to the rice, 1 cup at a time.

7. After 10 minutes, stir in the saffron. It will take about 20 minutes for the rice to absorb all the broth and to finish cooking. Remove pan from heat and stir in the remaining tablespoon of butter and the grated Parmesan cheese. Salt and pepper to taste. Arrange as in photo.

chicken breast "arlecchino"

PETTO DI POLLO ARLECCHINO

[6 SERVINGS]

6 chicken breasts

STUFFING

3 red peppers
6 slices prosciutto crudo
6 hearts of palm
  olive oil
  rosemary, sage, thyme, and
    unpeeled garlic
1 cup dry white wine
2 eggs
1 pound assorted vegetables

1. Spread out and pound the chicken breasts.

2. Roast the peppers in the oven or directly over high heat until they turn completely black. Then peel them, remove the caps, cut in half, and clean out seeds. Wash and pat dry.

3. Spread a slice of prosciutto crudo over each chicken breast; next, halve a red pepper and a heart of palm. Press the sides together and tie up like a roast.

4. Transfer to a preheated oven at 400° for about 30 minutes and roast in oil with the herbs and garlic. Discard garlic.

5. Add wine, ¼ cup at a time.

6. Make a "frittata" with the eggs and vegetables and serve as a side dish.

roasted baby chicken marinated with lemon, garlic, and thyme

GALLETTO CROCCANTE CON LIMONE, AGLIO E TIMO

[1 SERVING]

1 pound baby chicken
½ lemon, sliced
1 garlic clove
1 teaspoon fresh thyme, chopped
   salt and pepper, freshly ground
   olive oil
½ cup white wine
¼ cup brown sauce (see Basic
   Recipes, page 133)
3–4 ounces potatoes
   olive oil
   butter

GARNISH
garlic clove
thyme
tomato
mint

1. Cut the baby chicken in half, open it up, and flatten it out. Marinate overnight with lemon, garlic, thyme, salt, pepper, and a little oil.

2. Roast the chicken with olive oil in a preheated oven at 400° for about 20 minutes.

3. When cooked, remove meat and fat from the pan and add white wine. Reduce; add brown sauce and the thyme from the marinade.

4. Cut the chicken into 4 parts and pour sauce over it.

5. In the meantime, boil potatoes. When cooked, cut into rounds and sauté in oil and butter.

6. Display potatoes as in photo.

7. Dish can be decorated with garlic clove, a sprinkle of thyme, tomato, and mint.

103

breast of duck with lemon, honey, and pine nuts

PETTO DI ANATRA IN AGRO-DOLCE CON PINOLI

[1 SERVING]

4–5 ounces breast of duck
  olive oil
  juice of 1 lemon
2 teaspoons honey
¼ cup brown sauce (see Basic
  Recipes, page 133)
  butter
1 tablespoon pine nuts, toasted in
  butter
1 ounce ground meat
  olive oil
  butter
2 tablespoons white wine
1 tablespoon Parmesan cheese,
  grated
1 egg
1 zucchini blossom
3 ounces potatoes, baked in
  the oven until tender

GARNISH
  olives
1 slice lemon
  parsley

1. Sauté the duck breast in oil. When cooked, remove meat and fat and add the lemon juice.

2. Reduce. Add the honey; when it begins to caramelize, add the brown sauce. Continue cooking, and, at the last minute, add the butter to bind. Add the toasted pine nuts.

3. Slice the duck breast and fan out slices; pour the sauce over it.

4. Sauté the ground meat in oil and butter. Add wine and reduce. When the meat has cooled, blend with Parmesan and egg. Stuff the zucchini blossom with the meat mixture.

5. Arrange the zucchini blossom, lightly sautéed in oil and butter, and the potatoes, as in photo, together with all the garnishes.

calf's **brains** with **marinated** tomatoes

CERVELLA DORATA CON POMODORI MARINATI

[6 SERVINGS]

3½ ounces calf's brain (per person)
   lemon
2 eggs, beaten and seasoned
   bread crumbs
   olive oil and butter
18 plum tomatoes, sliced lengthwise
   and marinated (see Basic
   Recipes, page 133)
   fresh basil
   parsley, finely chopped

VEGETABLE FLAN
(See the ingredients in the
   recipe on page 100)
slices of carrot
slices of zucchini

1. Place brains in a bowl under cold running water and parboil in water and lemon. Drain and pat dry. Cut into discs (3 per person), dip in eggs, and cover with bread crumbs.

2. Sauté in oil and butter.

3. For the vegetable flans, prepare as directed in the recipe on page 100. Line 6 molds with slices of carrots and zucchini before pouring in the mixture.

4. Place the vegetable flan in the center of the plate, with the brains and tomatoes surrounding it.

5. Garnish with basil and parsley.

calf's **liver** venetian **style** with **polenta**

FEGATO ALLA VENEZIANA CON POLENTA

[6 SERVINGS]

1 pound onions
3 tablespoons olive oil
1 tablespoon butter
1¼ pounds calf's liver, thinly sliced
and cut up
3 or 4 fresh sage leaves (optional)
salt (as little as possible)

POLENTA

1¼ pounds finely ground cornmeal
1 tablespoon salt

1. Slice onions and cook over high heat in a large frying pan with oil and butter. After about 10 minutes, when onions start "sweating," add the liver and sage. Depending on the quality of the liver, it should take less than 3 minutes to cook. Continue cooking, adding the salt last; otherwise, the liver will become tough.

2. To cook polenta, use a large pot. Fill with 12 cups of water; salt and bring to a boil. Pour in the flour in a steady, slow stream and stir with a wooden spoon until it thickens. Let it cook slowly for at least 40 minutes; stir constantly.

3. Turn the polenta out on a wooden board or slab; shape with molds as in photo.

RIGHT: THE CANOVA ROOM

desserts

DOLCI

A selection of colorful drinks and a choice of ice cream, made on a daily basis in the hotel's pastry shop, photographed on the sundeck under the shade of the wisteria-covered gazebo.

The trompe-l'oeil façade in the background, constructed in 1856 and dedicated to Caroline of Brunswick, is known as the Queen of England building.

desserts

Panettone Filled with Ice Cream Served with Mascarpone and Chocolate Sauces
PANETTONE FARCITO CON SALSA DI MASCARPONE E CIOCCOLATO

Casanova's Delight
DESIDERIO DI CASANOVA

The Swans of Lake Como
I CIGNI DEL LAGO DI COMO

Tulips of Wild Berries
TULIPANO DI SOTTOBOSCO

Tarts with Berries and Strawberry Sauce
TRIS DI TARTELETTE AL FRUTTI DI BOSCO CON SALSA DI FRAGOLA

Crunchy Puff Pastry Grapes
GRAPPOLO DI BIGNOLE CROCCANTI

Meringues with Coffee Ice Cream in Caramel Sauce
MERINGHE CON GELATO AL CAFFÈ IN SALSA CARAMELLO

Tiramisù

Coffee Custard with Caramel Sauce
BUDINO AL CAFFÈ CON SALSA VANIGLIA

Lemon Tartlet with Vanilla Sauce
TORTINO AL LIMONE CON SALSA VANIGLIA

Puff Pastry with Wild Strawberries in a Strawberry Sauce
SFOGLIATINA ALLE FRAGOLE CON SALSA DI FRAGOLE

Fruit Mosaic
MOSAICO DI FRUTTA

Chocolate Christmas Tree Log
TRONCHETTO NATALIZIO

Shortcake with Fresh Fruits
CROSTATA DI FRUTTA DI STAGIONE

Napoleon
MILLEFOGLIE NAPOLEONE

Chocolate Cake
TORTA DI CIOCCOLATO

panettone filled with **ice cream** and **served** with **mascarpone** and **chocolate** sauces

PANETTONE FARCITO CON SALSA MASCARPONE E CIOCCOLATO

[6 SERVINGS]

one 1-pound panettone
  2 or 3 scoops of your favorite ice
    cream

CHOCOLATE SAUCE
  2 ounces chocolate
⅔ cup milk
  2 tablespoons sugar
  2 egg yolks, beaten

MASCARPONE SAUCE
  4 ounces fresh mascarpone
  2 egg yolks
  2 teaspoons sugar
  2 tablespoons cognac

1. Remove top and inner part of panettone, fill with ice cream, put top back on, and refrigerate.

2. Melt chocolate in a double boiler. Boil milk and mix with sugar and egg yolks. Add chocolate; whisk until smooth.

3. To make mascarpone sauce, combine listed ingredients.

4. Spread chocolate and mascarpone sauces on a plate; place a slice of panettone in the center.

casanova's delight

DESIDERIO DI CASANOVA

[6 SERVINGS]

BIGNÉ
2/3 cup water
2½ ounces butter
    pinch of salt
  1 cup flour
  3 eggs

PASTRY CREAM
  2 egg yolks
¼ cup sugar
1½ tablespoons flour
    vanilla, pinch (or vanilla bean)
2/3 cup milk

ICE CREAM MOUSSE
  6 egg yolks
  1 cup sugar
  1 pound whipped cream
    pistachio nuts, grated
3½ ounces strawberries
  1 tablespoon Grand Marnier liqueur

KIWI SAUCE
  1 pound kiwi
¾ cup sugar
    yogurt

1. Heat water with butter and salt. Add flour when butter has melted and stir with a wooden spoon until the batter forms a large blob. Remove from heat and allow to cool. Fold in the eggs, one at a time.

2. With a pastry bag, squeeze the dough onto an oiled baking sheet into 18 rounds, each the shape and size of a golf ball.

3. Place in a preheated oven at 400° for 15 minutes. Set aside to cool.

PASTRY CREAM
See Basic Recipes, page 134, for procedure.

ICE CREAM MOUSSE
1. Beat egg yolks with sugar in a double boiler. When frothy, remove from heat. When cool, gently fold into the whipped cream.

2. Divide into 3 parts: add to one the pistachio nuts; to the second, the strawberries; and to the third, the liqueur.

KIWI SAUCE
1. Blend the kiwi with the sugar to make the sauce.

2. On each dish spread the kiwi sauce and place yogurt around the perimeter. Halve the bignés and fill each bottom half with the ice cream mousses and fill the upper half with the pastry cream. Then put the 2 parts together again. Arrange the bignés and decorate, as in photo.

• *Bigné* is the Italianization of the French *beignet*.

112

the **swans** of **lake como**

I CIGNI DEL LAGO DI COMO

[6 SERVINGS]

gelatin
blue and green food coloring
puff pastry
zabaione (see below)
2 squares dark chocolate

PUFF PASTRY

2½ cups water
1½ pounds butter
1 vanilla bean
½ teaspoon salt
2½ cups flour
8-10 eggs, depending on size

ZABAIONE

8 egg yolks
1¼ cups sugar
2 cups dry Marsala
1 cup dry white wine
1 lemon rind, grated
½ orange rind, grated
3 cups heavy whipping cream

1. Dissolve a package of gelatin and add the coloring. Pour onto a large platter. Refrigerate.

2. In a large saucepan, heat water with butter, vanilla bean, and salt. When butter has melted, remove bean. Stir in the flour with a wooden spoon until the batter forms a large blob and comes away from the sides of the pan. Remove from stove and cool. Fold in the eggs, one at a time. With a pastry bag, squeeze the dough in the shape of pears (will yield 12) onto an oiled baking sheet. These will be the swans' bodies. On another sheet, form a dozen swans' heads and necks, shaped like the number 2. The necks will be ready in 20 minutes, the bodies in 30–35 minutes.

3. Meanwhile, make the zabaione. In a double boiler, whisk egg yolks and sugar until frothy and creamy. Pour in the Marsala, the wine, and the grated fruit rinds, increasing temperature of water. Continue beating until mixture has a smooth consistency. Remove from heat and place over ice cubes to cool. In the meantime, whip the cream; blend gently into the zabaione.

4. Cut the top off from each of the swans' bodies and set the cut-off portion aside. Fill the hollow part with the zabaione. Take the necks and place them into the zabaione upright. Take the reserved top parts and cut them in half crosswise. Place these into the filling behind the necks to form the wings. Place the swans on the gelatin lake. Melt the chocolate. Squirt the melted chocolate through a cone of waxed paper onto a sheet of waxed paper to form fences. As soon as the chocolate hardens place the fences around the lake.

tulips of wild berries

TULIPANO DI SOTTOBOSCO

[6 SERVINGS]

3 ounces butter, softened
3 ounces powdered sugar
3 egg whites, beaten
3 ounces flour

ZABAIONE

3 egg yolks
⅓ cup sugar
¼ cup orange juice
¼ cup dry white wine
   raspberries
   mulberries
   strawberries, halved
   blueberries

APRICOT SAUCE

1½ pounds apricots
½ cup sugar
1 tablespoon cornstarch

GARNISH

yogurt

1. Mix butter with sugar.

2. Gently fold in the egg whites, then the flour. With a spoon, drop 6 mounds on a well-greased and floured baking dish. With a fork, give them a round shape. Bake in preheated oven at 400° for 12 minutes.

3. While still hot, press center of each mound with an overturned cup to give it the shape of a tulip with open petals.

ZABAIONE

1. In a double boiler, whisk egg yolks with sugar.

2. Add orange juice and wine. Keep beating until smooth and rich in consistency. Remove from heat and continue beating until cool.

3. Fill the tulip petals with the berries, cover with the zabaione, and place under broiler for a couple of minutes.

APRICOT SAUCE

1. To make the sauce, blend the apricots with the sugar; then bring to a boil with the cornstarch.

2. When cool, spread the apricot sauce on each plate, decorate with yogurt (as in photo), and place the tulips in the center.

tarts with berries and strawberry sauce

TRIS DI TARTELETTE AI FRUTTI DI BOSCO CON SALSA DI FRAGOLA

[6 SERVINGS]

4 ounces butter
½ cup sugar
2 egg yolks
½ teaspoon lemon rind, grated
1¼ cups flour

PASTRY CREAM

1 cup milk
3 egg yolks
¼ cup sugar
1½ tablespoons flour
vanilla, pinch of powder or drop
   of liquid
¼ teaspoon lemon rind, grated

STRAWBERRY SAUCE

1 pound strawberries
½ cup sugar
1 teaspoon cornstarch

FRUIT

2 ounces kiwi
6 large strawberries
1 mango
2 ounces blueberries

yogurt
pistachio ice cream

1. Combine butter and sugar in a bowl.

2. Add the egg yolks, lemon rind, and the flour. Mix and knead lightly with fingertips. Shape into a ball and chill for about 30 minutes.

3. Roll out, divide into 18 pieces, and press the pastry into boat-shaped molds. Prick the pastry with a fork and place in preheated oven at 400° for 15 minutes.

PASTRY CREAM
See Basic Recipes, page 134, for procedure.

STRAWBERRY SAUCE
1. Blend the strawberries with the sugar; boil mixture with the cornstarch.

2. When cool, spread the sauce on each plate. Decorate with yogurt.

3. Fill the pastry boats with the pastry cream and the fruit, as in photo.

4. Decorate with pistachio ice cream and more fruit.

crunchy puff **pastry** grapes

GRAPPOLO DI BIGNOLE CROCCANTI

[6 SERVINGS]

BIGNÉ

1 cup water
7 tablespoons butter
salt, pinch
⅓ cup flour
4 eggs

PASTRY CREAM

1¾ cups milk
7 egg yolks
1 cup sugar
¾ cup flour
almonds, toasted and grated
2 tablespoons Aurum liqueur

CARAMEL SAUCE

1 cup water
1½ cups sugar

GARNISH

1½ cups cream, whipped
green food coloring

1. Heat the water with butter and salt. Add flour when butter has melted and stir with a wooden spoon until the batter forms a large blob. Remove from heat and allow to cool. Fold in the eggs, one at a time.

2. With a pastry bag, squeeze the dough in the shape of tiny balls onto an oiled baking sheet. Place in a preheated oven at 400° for 15 minutes. Set aside to cool.

PASTRY CREAM

1. See Basic Recipes, page 134, for procedure.

2. Add almonds. When bignés are cooled, squirt some of the pastry cream into each bigné through a small hole.

CARAMEL SAUCE

1. Boil water with sugar until it is caramelized. Remove from heat and wait 2 minutes before dipping each bigné into the caramel sauce.

2. On a marble countertop that has been brushed with oil, spread remaining caramel sauce. Add food coloring and cut out leaves to use for garnish, as in photo.

3. Add 2 tablespoons of Aurum to remaining pastry cream and mix.

4. Spread pastry cream on each plate and arrange the bignés like a bunch of grapes; complete with green leaves. Use the whipped cream to cover the little holes in between the bignés.

meringues with coffee ice cream in caramel sauce

MERINGHE CON GELATO AL CAFFÈ IN SALSA CARAMELLO

[6 SERVINGS]

5 egg whites
1½ cups sugar
 vanilla, pinch of powder or drop
 of liquid
¼ teaspoon lemon juice
 powdered sugar
3 semisweet chocolate squares

COFFEE ICE CREAM

6 egg yolks
½ cup sugar
2 cups milk, heated
1 cup espresso coffee

CARAMEL SAUCE

¼ cup water
½ cup sugar
1½ cups cream

GARNISH
 pistachios, chopped
 candied fruit
 whipped cream
 chocolate ornaments
 yogurt
 melted chocolate

1. Beat the egg whites until somewhat stiff; add sugar, then vanilla and lemon juice. Beat until stiff. Grease the bottom of a baking dish with butter and sprinkle with flour.

2. With a pastry bag, pipe 18 (or more) meringues shaped as in photo. Sprinkle with powdered sugar and bake in oven at 300° for about 3 hours.

3. Melt chocolate in a double boiler and dip in half (9) the meringues.

COFFEE ICE CREAM
1. Beat egg yolks with sugar in a bowl.

2. Add heated milk in a slow steady stream, beating vigorously with a wire whisk.

3. Add coffee. Freeze in an ice cream machine.

CARAMEL SAUCE
1. Boil the water with sugar until it caramelizes. Add cream and bring to a boil. Remove and cool.

2. Spread caramel sauce on each plate and decorate with yogurt and chocolate.

3. Place a scoop of the coffee ice cream between one white meringue and one chocolate meringue and arrange over the caramel sauce, as in photo, together with the garnishes.

tiramisù

[6 SERVINGS]

2 egg yolks
2 tablespoons sugar
½ pound mascarpone
2 egg whites
6 ounces cream, whipped
3 cups espresso coffee mixed with
    1 tablespoon brandy
1 (7-ounce) package savoiardi
    (ladyfingers)
3 tablespoons cocoa powder

CREAM SAUCE
3 ounces heavy cream, mixed with
    6 tablespoons pastry cream
1 cup milk
⅓ cup sugar
2 eggs
    vanilla, pinch of powder or drop
    of liquid
⅛ teaspoon lemon peel, grated
⅛ teaspoon orange peel, grated

GARNISH
melted chocolate
strawberry sauce (see page 115)

1. Beat egg yolks with sugar. Add mascarpone and mix. Beat egg whites until stiff. Gently fold the egg whites into the mascarpone mixture. Last, stir in the whipped cream.

2. Set aside one quarter portion of this mixture. Quickly dip the ladyfingers into coffee and brandy. Line 6 molds with about half of the ladyfingers.

3. Fill the molds with mascarpone and whipped cream mixture and cover with the remaining ladyfingers. Chill for at least an hour.

4. Turn over the molds. Cover with the reserved mascarpone mixture.

5. Sprinkle with cocoa powder.

PASTRY CREAM
1. See Basic Recipes, page 134, for procedure.

2. Spread cream sauce on each plate. Place tiramisù in the center and decorate as in photo.

coffee **custard** with **caramel** sauce

BUDINO AL CAFFÈ CON SALSA CARAMELLO

[6 SERVINGS]

CARAMEL SAUCE
3 tablespoons water
1½ cups sugar
1½ cups hot milk
3 egg yolks
1 tablespoon sugar

CUSTARD
2½ cups cream
3½ ounces powdered sugar
3 cups espresso coffee
1½ sheets gelatin (isinglass),
   softened in cold water

GARNISH
whipped cream
chocolate, melted
strawberry sauce (see page 115)

CARAMEL SAUCE

1. Boil water with the 1½ cups sugar. When it turns golden, remove a little of the caramel with a spoon to cover the bottom of 6 (2-in. diameter) molds. Then add hot milk to the pan in a slow and steady stream. Bring to a boil.

2. In the meantime, beat egg yolks with the tablespoon of sugar.

3. Remove the milk and caramel mixture from heat and pour into a bowl; mix with the egg yolk mixture.

4. Return above to a saucepan and heat without bringing to a boil and stir until it reaches a creamy consistency. Cool.

CUSTARD

1. Boil cream, powdered sugar, coffee, and gelatin.

2. Fill the molds with the custard and chill for 3–4 hours.

3. Spread the caramel sauce on each plate. Place the coffee custard in the center.

4. Use the whipped cream, melted chocolate, and strawberry sauce to decorate, as in photo.

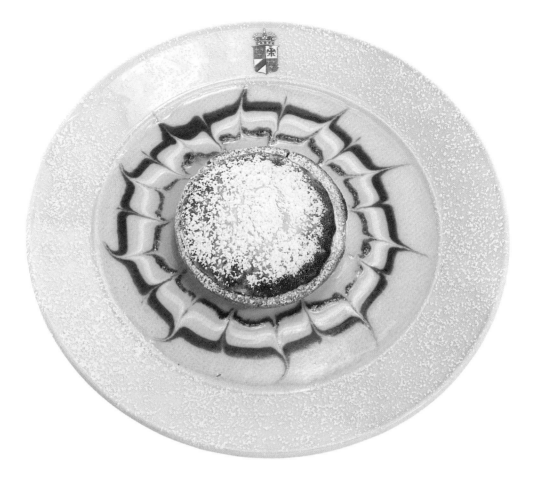

lemon **tartlet** with **vanilla** sauce

TORTINO AL LIMONE CON SALSA VANIGLIA

[6 SERVINGS]

SHORTCAKE
3½ ounces flour
1¼ ounces sugar
     pinch salt
1¾ ounces butter
  1 egg yolk
  ⅛ teaspoon lemon rind, grated

LEMON CUSTARD
  2 ounces sugar
1½ ounces butter, softened
     juice of 1 lemon
  2 egg yolks
  2 egg whites, beaten until stiff
     powdered sugar

VANILLA SAUCE
1½ cups hot milk
  1 vanilla bean
  4 egg yolks
  ⅓ cup sugar

GARNISH
     whipped cream
     melted chocolate
     strawberry sauce (see page 115)
     powdered sugar

SHORTCAKE
1. See page 124 for shortcake procedure.

2. Fill 6 (3½ in. diameter) molds with the shortcake pastry. Bake for 10 minutes at 425°. Cool and remove from molds.

LEMON CUSTARD
1. In a double boiler, whisk sugar, butter, lemon juice, and egg yolks until mixture has consistency of mayonnaise.

2. When cool, add the egg whites. Fill the tartlets with the custard and return to the oven for 5–10 minutes, until they rise like soufflés.

3. Remove from oven and sprinkle with the powdered sugar.

VANILLA SAUCE
1. Boil milk and vanilla bean in a saucepan.

2. In a bowl, beat the egg yolks with the sugar.

3. Remove the vanilla bean. Pour hot milk in a steady stream into the egg and sugar mixture and return to the stove. Stir without bringing to a boil. Cool quickly by placing the saucepan over ice cubes.

4. Spread vanilla sauce on plates, and place the tartlets in the center. Decorate as in photo and cover the plate with a sprinkling of powdered sugar.

puff **pastry** with **wild** strawberries in a **strawberry** sauce

SFOGLIATINA ALLE FRAGOLINE IN SALSA DI FRAGOLE

[6 SERVINGS]

2 pounds puff pastry

PASTRY CREAM
1½ cups milk
½ cup sugar
4 egg yolks
⅓ cup flour
    vanilla, pinch of powder or drop
      of liquid
    lemon rind

"LINGUE DI GATTO" COOKIES
2 tablespoons butter, softened
¼ cup powdered sugar
1 egg white, beaten
¼ cup flour
    vanilla, pinch of powder or drop
      of liquid

STRAWBERRY SAUCE
1 pound strawberries
⅓ cup sugar
¼ teaspoon cornstarch

GARNISH
¾ pound wild strawberries
    pistachio ice cream
    melted chocolate (optional)

1. Roll out the puff pastry as thin as possible. With a knife, cut out 6 leaves shaped as in photo. Prick with a fork and set aside for one hour.

2. Bake for 15 minutes at 400°.

PASTRY CREAM
See Basic Recipes, page 134, for procedure.

"LINGUE DI GATTO" COOKIES
1. Mix softened butter with powdered sugar. Gently fold in the beaten egg white, then the flour and vanilla. Pick up the mixture with a spoon and place, on a greased and floured baking dish, small well-spaced mounds.

2. Bake for 10 minutes at 400°.

STRAWBERRY SAUCE
1. Blend the strawberries with the sugar. Boil with the cornstarch.

2. Spread the sauce on each plate. Place a puff pastry leaf on one side of the plate, and fill it with the pastry cream, with the strawberries on top.

3. Decorate with a scoop of pistachio ice cream placed over a cookie. Garnish with sliced strawberries or strawberries dipped in chocolate.

fruit mosaic

MOSAICO DI FRUTTA

[6 SERVINGS]

grapefruit
mulberries
raspberries
banana
wild strawberries
kiwi
mango
papaya

Italians generally finish their meals with fruit, which they prefer to a dessert. At Villa d'Este, if you ask for a fruit assortment, this is an example of how it may be presented to you.

For clients with a sweet tooth, a scoop of a favorite ice cream or a fruit sorbet can be added in the center.

At Villa d'Este, the ice cream is homemade, and the chocolate ice cream is especially scrumptious!

chocolate christmas-tree log

TRONCHETTO NATALIZIO

[6 SERVINGS]

5 eggs
¾ cup sugar
1½ cups flour
¼ teaspoon vanilla
1 teaspoon lemon rind, grated

CHOCOLATE CREAM

7 ounces butter
⅔ cup sugar
4 tablespoons powdered cocoa
1 cup Aurum liqueur

GARNISH

9 semisweet chocolate squares
    (1 ounce each) for icing
1 tablespoon whipped cream
2 tablespoons almond paste
1 tablespoon grated green
    pistachio

1. Beat the eggs with the sugar; add the flour, vanilla, and lemon rind.

2. Roll out the dough, ⅛ inch thick, on greased foil. Place in a preheated oven at 425° for 10 minutes.

3. Whisk butter and sugar. Add cocoa and Aurum to make the chocolate cream. In the meantime, the dough with have settled. Turn upside-down and remove foil.

4. With a brush, spread liqueur over half the chocolate cream; roll dough and freeze for 2 hours.

5. Cut obliquely the 2 ends of the log, spread the remaining chocolate cream (reserving one tablespoon) over the roll, and shape into 2 or 3 branches, as in photo. Again, place the roll in the freezer for about an hour.

6. In a double boiler, melt the chocolate squares.

7. When cool, spread the melted chocolate over the log and cover the log ends and the branches with whipped cream.

8. Use chocolate cream and melted chocolate in a pastry bag to decorate, as in photo. Garnish with mushrooms shaped from the almond paste. Sprinkle with pistachio.

shortcake with fresh fruits

CROSTATA DI FRUTTA DI STAGIONE

[6 SERVINGS]

SHORTCAKE
7 ounces flour
2½ ounces sugar
pinch salt
3½ ounces butter
2 egg yolks
¼ teaspoon lemon rind, grated

PASTRY CREAM
3 egg yolks
⅓ cup sugar
2 ounces flour
vanilla, pinch of powder or drop
of liquid
1½ cups milk

FILLING
strawberries or other fresh fruit
apricot jam

1. Sift together flour, sugar, and salt on a wooden pastry board. Make a well in the center; add butter, egg yolks, and lemon rind. Mix and knead with fingertips, taking care not to handle too much. When smooth, shape into a ball and chill for about 30 minutes.

2. Roll out lightly in a circle, cut edges, and keep dough about 1 inch larger than a 9-inch (diameter) fluted pastry tin.

3. Butter and flour the pan; fit pastry into it. Again, trim the edges, prick with fork, and flute edges.

4. Place in preheated oven at 325° for 15–20 minutes.

PASTRY CREAM
1. See Basic Recipes, page 134, for procedure.

2. When pastry cream is cool, spread evenly on the bottom of the shortcake.

3. Fill with whatever fresh fruits are available. Glaze with an apricot jam, melted with a little hot water.

napoleon cake

MILLEFOGLIE NAPOLEONE

[6 SERVINGS]

2 pounds puff pastry

PASTRY CREAM

2 cups milk
1 cup sugar
5 egg yolks
½ cup flour, heaped
  vanilla, pinch of powder or drop
    of liquid
1 teaspoon lemon rind, grated
1 tablespoon brandy

GARNISH
  powdered sugar
  melted chocolate for decoration

1. Roll out the puff pastry as thin as possible. Cut out 18 discs, each with a diameter of 3½ inches.

2. Place the discs on a baking dish; set aside for one hour.

3. Place discs in a preheated oven at 400° for 15 minutes.

PASTRY CREAM

1. See Basic Recipes, page 134, for procedure.

2. Remove one quarter of the pastry cream and to it add the brandy. Spread on each plate.

3. Prepare the cakes by coating 6 discs with the remaining pastry cream; continue to add discs and pastry cream, totaling 3 layers for each cake. Sprinkle the top disc with powdered sugar.

4. Decorate the cake and sauce with the melted chocolate.

chocolate cake

TORTA DI CIOCCOLATO

[6 SERVINGS]

SPONGE CAKE

5 egg yolks
¾ cup sugar
5 egg whites
1 cup flour
1 cup potato flour
   vanilla, pinch of powder or drop
      of liquid

PASTRY CREAM

2½ cups milk
⅔ cup sugar
⅓ cup flour
6 egg yolks
   vanilla, pinch
¼ teaspoon lemon rind, grated
3 tablespoons cocoa
½ cup rum
   water and sugar
7 or 8 squares (1 ounce each)
   semisweet chocolate
   powdered sugar

1. Beat the egg yolks with the sugar. Separately beat the egg whites until stiff. Gently fold the egg yolks into the egg whites; when well blended, mix in the flour and the vanilla.

2. Place the batter in 6 (3½-inch diameter) molds, well greased and coated with flour.

3. Bake in a preheated oven at 375° for 15 minutes. Remove from oven and cool.

4. For the pastry cream, see Basic Recipes, page 134. At the last moment, add the cocoa.

5. Slice each cake crosswise into 3 parts. Dip each part in the rum, diluted with water and sugar.

6. Spread chocolate pastry cream between the layers and on top. With a knife, scrape the semisweet chocolate over each cake and sprinkle with the powdered sugar.

RIGHT: THE NAPOLEON ROOM IS USED
FOR SMALL, PRIVATE PARTIES

basic recipes

A display of the wide variety of cheeses typical of the Lombardy region and surrounding areas.

basic recipes

chicken broth

BRODO DI POLLO

3–4 pound chicken
4 quarts cold water
1 tablespoon coarse salt
1 bay leaf
2 carrots
1 medium onion
1 leek
2 celery stalks without leaves

1. Place chicken in a large pot and cover with water. Add salt and bay leaf. Cover and slowly bring to a boil, skim with a slotted ladle and add whole carrots, onion, leek, and celery stalks.

2. Simmer for an hour and a half. Filter broth through a carefully wrung cheesecloth soaked in cold water. Can be refrigerated for a few days but should be boiled daily for about 10 minutes.

3. If planning to freeze broth, remove chicken when it is cooked and the vegetables. Leave the pot uncovered and on a high flame; reduce by half the liquid. When cool, strain into containers and store in freezer.
Same procedure is used for capon.

beef broth

BRODO DI MANZO

2 pounds stewing beef (shin or brisket)
4 quarts cold water
1 tablespoon coarse salt
1 bay leaf
2 carrots
1 medium onion
1 leek
2 celery stalks without leaves

Follow the same procedure as in chicken broth, above, substituting beef for chicken.

fish broth

BRODO DI PESCE

bay leaf, parsley, and thyme sprigs
bones and trimmings of fish (sole, turbot, etc.)
onion, carrot, celery, and leek, coarsely chopped
2 cups water
2 cups white wine
salt and pepper to taste

1. Place all aromatics at the bottom of the pot.

2. Cover with fish bones and trimmings.

3. Add vegetables, water, and wine.

4. Bring to a boil, skim, and cook slowly for 30 minutes.

5. Strain through a fine sieve. Add salt and pepper to taste.

131

court bouillon

2 cups white wine
5 cups water
1 onion, chopped
1 carrot, chopped
  bay leaf
6 peppercorns
2 whole lemons, sliced
  sprigs of parsley
½ teaspoon fennel seeds
  salt

Place all ingredients in a large pot, bring to a boil, and cook for 30 minutes. Strain and use as needed.

white sauce

BESCIAMELLA

MAKES 2 CUPS

4 tablespoons butter
3 tablespoons flour
2 cups milk, heated
  pinch salt
  nutmeg, freshly grated

1. Melt butter over low flame, and mix in flour by stirring with a wooden spoon.

2. Cook for 2 minutes, then gradually start adding heated milk, stirring constantly until the sauce is smooth.

3. Season with salt and nutmeg, and simmer for a few minutes, until the sauce has a creamy consistency.

tomato sauce

SALSA DI POMODORO

1 small red onion, coarsely chopped
4 tablespoons olive oil
1 bay leaf
2 pounds fresh ripe Italian plum
    tomatoes or 28-ounce can
    peeled plum tomatoes
  salt and black pepper, freshly
    ground
  pinch sugar (optional)
2 or 3 fresh basil leaves

1. Chop the tomatoes in the blender.

2. Simmer the onion in the olive oil until it turns golden; add tomatoes and bay leaf.

3. Season lightly with salt and pepper.

4. When tasting, if you find that the sauce is a little bitter, you can add a pinch of sugar.

5. Simmer and stir occasionally with a wooden spoon for about a half hour, until the sauce is no longer watery. Add basil. Remove the bay leaf.

marinated **tomatoes**

POMODORI MARINATI

fresh plum tomatoes
olive oil
basil leaves
salt

1. Cut off the tops of the tomatoes and parboil the tomatoes.

2. Peel; remove seeds and liquid.

3. Dice or cut lengthwise, and marinate in olive oil with the basil and a little salt for about an hour.

meat sauce

SUGO DI CARNE

1 onion, chopped
1 carrot, chopped
1 celery stalk, chopped
2 tablespoons olive oil
2 tablespoons butter
2 pounds ground beef
½ cup dried mushrooms, soaked in
    warm water and strained
    salt and pepper to taste
2 tablespoons parsley, chopped
1 cup dry red wine
2 tablespoons tomato paste
1 can (28-ounce) Italian peeled
    tomatoes, chopped
1 tablespoon dried herbs
    (marjoram, oregano, thyme, etc.)
1–2 cups beef broth

1. Over a medium flame, sauté onion, carrot, and celery in oil and butter until the onion turns golden.

2. Add the meat, mushrooms, salt, pepper, and parsley. Cook slowly.

3. Turn heat to high and pour in the wine. When it has almost evaporated, lower the flame and add the tomato paste, tomatoes, and dried herbs.

4. Stir occasionally and simmer for at least an hour (the longer, the better); add a little broth at a time to keep the sauce from reducing.

brown **sauce**

FONDO BRUNO

2–3 pounds beef and veal bones, cut
    into small pieces
1 pound leg of beef or shoulder,
    cut up
2 carrots, chopped
2 onions, chopped
1 celery stalk, chopped
½ cup red wine
    bouquet of fresh herbs: parsley,
    sage, rosemary, thyme, and
    bay leaf

1. Place bones and meat in a shallow pan and place in a preheated oven at 400°, until browned. Add the carrots, onions, and celery, and leave in the oven until the vegetables become seasoned and slightly wilted.

2. Remove pan from oven and remove bones, meat, and vegetables with a slotted ladle to drip off any fat.

3. Place in a large pot, heat, pour in the wine, and evaporate.

4. Add cold water to fill the pot and bring to a boil. Add the bouquet of herbs. Lower the heat and simmer for about 3 hours. Skim occasionally with a slotted spoon. Reduce the liquid to about half the initial quantity. Strain through a fine sieve and let cool.

5. For a richer sauce, cook liquid and reduce until thick. The sauce can be kept in the refrigerator for at least a week or frozen in ice-cube containers for a couple of months.

mayonnaise

MAIONESE

1 egg
1 tablespoon lemon juice
½ teaspoon salt
1 cup olive oil

1. Break egg into blender; add lemon juice and salt.

2. Add enough oil to cover blades. Cover and turn motor on low speed for a few seconds. Uncover with motor running and pour in remaining oil in a steady stream.

homemade pasta

PASTA FRESCA

[6-8 SERVINGS]

4 cups flour
5 eggs
1 pinch salt
2 tablespoons olive oil

1. Pour the flour in a mound on a wooden, marble, or Formica surface, make a well in the middle and break in the eggs, salt, and oil. Beat the eggs lightly with a fork and start mixing the flour into the eggs in a circular movement with your fingers. Use one hand for mixing; with the other hand, push the flour into the center; keep working until you have obtained a well combined, doughy ball.

2. Sprinkle both surface and hands with flour and begin kneading by pushing the pasta away from you. Continue until the pasta is quite elastic and doesn't break off when you pull. Sprinkle with flour, cover with a damp cloth, and let rest for a couple of hours in a cool place.

3. If the ball is too big to handle, divide it up into 2 or 3 pieces. To thin out the pieces, use a rolling pin.

4. First roll out the dough, then roll and stretch at the same time around the rolling pin. Repeat about 12 times. If you have a pasta machine, use it instead of the rolling pin. Each time, sprinkle lightly with flour. At this stage, the dough should be as thin as a piece of cloth. Cut the dough into any size or shape you desire.

5. To make green pasta, add 6 ounces of cooked, strained, and finely chopped spinach to the eggs.

pastry cream

CREMA PASTICCERA

egg yolks
sugar
flour
vanilla (a pinch of powder or a
    drop of liquid
milk
lemon rind (optional)

Quantities of above ingredients
are indicated in the individual
recipes.

1. Mix egg yolks, sugar, and flour in a saucepan.

2. Add vanilla.

3. Heat milk with lemon rind. When milk comes to a boil, remove rind.

4. Pour heated milk in a slow steady stream into the egg, sugar, and flour mixture. Cook on a low flame until the mixture thickens, whisking constantly; do not overboil.

5. Let cool.

conversion chart

LIQUID MEASURES

FLUID OUNCES	U.S. MEASURES	IMPERIAL MEASURES	MILLILITERS
	1 tsp	1 tsp	5
¼	2 tsp	1 dessert spoon	7
½	1 tbs	1 tbs	15
1	2 tbs	2 tbs	28
2	¼ cup	4 tbs	56
4	½ cup or ¼ pint	110	
5		¼ pint or 1 gill	140
6	¾ cup		170
8	1 cup or ½ pint		225
9			250, ¼ liter
10	1¼ cups	½ pint	280
12	1½ cups or ¾ pint	340	
15		¾ pint	420
16	2 cups or 1 pint		450
18	2¼ cups		500
20	2½ cups	1 pint	560
24	3 cups or 1½ pints		675
25		1¼ pints	700
27	3½ cups		750
30	3¾ cups	1½ pints	840
32	4 cups or 2 pints or 1 quart		900
35		1¾ pints	980
36	4½ cups		1000, 1 liter
40	5 cups or 2½ pints	2 pints or 1 quart	
48	6 cups or 3 pints		1350
50		2½ pints	1400
60	7½ cups	3 pints	1680
64	8 cups or 4 pints or 2 quarts		1800
72	9 cups		2000, 2 liters
80	10 cups or 5 pints	4 pints	2250
96	12 cups or 3 quarts		2700
100		5 pints	2800

SOLID MEASURES

U.S. AND IMPERIAL MEASURES

OUNCES	POUNDS	GRAMS	KILOS
1		28	
2		56	
3½		100	
4	¼	100	
5		140	
6		168	
8	½	225	
9		250	¼
12	¾	340	
16	1	450	
18		500	½
20	1¼	560	
24	1½	675	
27		750	¾
28	1¾	780	
32	2	900	
36	2¼	1000	1
40	2½	1100	
48	3	1350	
54		1500	1½
64	4	1800	
72	4½	2000	2
80	5	2250	2¼
90		2500	2½
100	6	2800	2¾

OVEN TEMPERATURE EQUIVALENTS

FAHRENHEIT	GAS MARK	CELSIUS	HEAT OF OVEN
225	¼	105	very cool
250	½	120	very cool
275	1	135	cool
300	2	150	cool
325	3	160	moderate
350	4	175	moderate
375	5	190	fairly hot
400	6	200	fairly hot
425	7	222	hot
450	8	230	very hot
475	9	245	very hot

index